WHITE   RED

WHITE RED BLACK.

SKETCHES OF SOCIETY

IN

THE UNITED STATES

DURING

THE VISIT OF THEIR GUEST.

BY

FRANCIS AND THERESA PULSZKY.

IN THREE VOLUMES.

VOL. I.

NEGRO UNIVERSITIES PRESS
NEW YORK

Originally published in 1853 by Trubner and Co.

Reprinted in 1968
by Negro Universities Press
A DIVISION OF GREENWOOD PUBLISHING CORP
New York

Library of Congress Catalogue Card Number: 68-58066

PREFACE.

MANY books on America have been published in England;—earnest and satirical accounts, serious and flippant narratives, caricatures and sketches, bird's-eye views, and finished pictures. Miss Martineau, Silk Buckingham, George Combe, Alexander Mackay, Sir Charles Lyell, have treated in their valuable works the most different phases of American life. Why then another book, on a subject so often and, in some quarters, so ably treated? The question is easily answered. America is growing rapidly, and changes its aspect unceasingly; a short time gives to the States a different appearance, and a picture, true to-day, after a couple of years no longer bears resemblance. And then, the Americans are so closely related to the English, as they speak the same language, and live under the same common law, that some of the tourists have been induced to direct their attention less to the working of the different institutions, than to insignificant discrepancies on the surface of society. A foreigner, strange to both countries, without previous predilection for, or prejudice against, either of them, can, perhaps, be more impartial in his views of the United States, than the son of the mother-country, attached to her manners and customs. These reasons have induced me to carry an owl to Athens, by publishing these volumes.

The work is, perhaps, not so superfluous as it seems at first sight, as many incorrect notions on American institutions are still prevailing on this side the ocean. A year has hardly elapsed since an English Under-Secretary of State for Foreign Affairs provoked ridicule in the United States, by mentioning in Parliament "the delicacy of relations between the central and *provincial* (sic) governments of the United States." In fact, he showed himself unaware that full constitutional remedies are already provided in the States, for the inconveniences of which he complained. In the same way the English public has been accustomed to underrate the development of America, and the character of her citizens, except in regard to commerce.

The peculiar opportunities which we enjoyed in travelling over the United States with Kossuth, the guest of the nation, afforded us more facility of becoming familiar with the policy and society of the New World, than is granted to most travellers. We became personally acquainted with nearly all the leading men of the States, and the frankness and communicativeness, natural to the American character, allowed us to get a deeper insight, through our friends, into the workings of republican self-government, as well as of party politics.

Mrs. Pulszky kept a regular Diary, the greater part of which has been incorporated with this publication. We did not dwell upon many particulars of American manners and habits, which often strike English travellers. For example, we were not shocked that, at breakfast, the Americans pour the contents of their eggs into glasses; we did not enquire whether the orthodoxy of eating lamb with mint-sauce, roast beef with Yorkshire pudding, and rhubarb pie with Devonshire cream, has survived the declaration of American Independence; we do not know, whether " the American attempts at steaks and chops" are ridiculous or not, not being accustomed to attach peculiar importance to the philosophy of the kitchen and the dining-room, and convinced, by experience, that no nation in the world possesses the monopoly of good cookery. Belonging to an eminently smoking people, the extensive use of the cigar did not hurt my feelings, though I thought that chewing and its consequences were no improvements on the use of the fragrant leaf.

In regard to graver matters, I do not evade any question, though slavery, for instance, is a point on which it is difficult to write, without giving offence on one or the other side of the Atlantic. The English are so proud because they have ceased to be slaveholders nearly a whole score of years, that they overlook the difficulties with which this question is connected in the Union; whilst the Americans of the South are so touchy in regard to the sovereignty of their States, that they call even the modest publications of a tourist, a "foreign intervention" in their domestic concerns, and, by the very fact, excite the resentment of those who feel no sympathy with the "peculiar institution." I give my opinion openly, without seeking to ingratiate myself with any party. In the same way I attempted to describe the large contending political parties and their subdivisions, and the different aspect of society in the four great portions of the Union, faithfully and conscientiously. We met friends amongst all the sections of the United States; I was convinced of the earnestness and sincerity of all the parties, and I give their principles without attempting to decide which of them is more conducive to the weal of the country. As far as I venture to form an opinion, it is, that the extinction of either of these great parties would be a national calamity.

Though I accompanied Kossuth on his journey through the different States of the Union, he is in no way, and in no point, responsible for any of the views which I take. His views on America have been expressed in his speeches.

The Three Letters of a New England Lady to Mrs. Pulszky, on American Character and Education, given in the Appendix of the third volume, are such valuable sketches of American life, that, with the permission of the writer, I have adorned these volumes with them.

FRANCIS PULSZKY.

BAYSWATER,
     February, 1853.

CONTENTS OF VOL. I.

CHAPTER I.

PASSAGE TO AMERICA.

Page

1. Departure from England 1
2. Discovery of America before Columbus . . . 5
3. The Americans in Europe 12
4. Escape of Madame Kossuth 17
5. Turkish Hospitality 45

CHAPTER II.

STATEN ISLAND, NEW YORK CITY.

1. Arrival at Staten Island 51
2. Reception in New York 64
3. New York Society, Architecture, and Meetings . . . 75
4. The Periodical Press in New York City . . . 102
5. Titles and Nicknames in the United States . . . 108

CHAPTER III.

COLONISATION—PHYSICAL AND POLITICAL CONFIGURATION OF THE UNITED STATES—PARTIES, AND THEIR SUBDIVISIONS.

1. Colonisation 113
2. Physical Configuration of North America . . . 127
3. Political Configuration of the United States . . 142
4. American Parties and their Principles 158

CHAPTER IV.

PHILADELPHIA—BALTIMORE.

Page

1. Philadelphia—The Reception—Mrs. Mott—The Prison—
   Independence Hall   189
2. Great Men of Philadelphia   202
3. Baltimore   214

CHAPTER V.

WASHINGTON CITY.

1. Society   218
2. Site of the City—Politics   231
3. Kossuth and the Congress—Banquets—the Monuments of
   Washington City   244

APPENDIX.

THE NORTHMEN IN NORTH AMERICA.

WHITE, RED, AND BLACK.

CHAPTER I.

PASSAGE TO AMERICA.

I. DEPARTURE FROM ENGLAND.

On the 20th of November, early in the morning,
we left London and proceeded to Southampton.
About a month had elapsed since Kossuth had
landed there, and was received as no other foreigner
ever has been received in England. A short month
had won golden opinions for him all over the
country. In spite of the increasing hostility of the
most influential organ of the press, he had found
many a hearty friend of his cause, and many an
enthusiastic admirer of his person here, where he
sought but a temporary asylum for his children. The
power of his eloquence had silenced many of those to
whom his openly avowed principles were at least
unseasonable, and, though a foreigner, he had the ear
of the public. His stay in England was an unin-
terrupted triumph unexpected to him; in our selfish
prosaic age, it seemed like a tale of the 'Arabian
Nights.' His friends in Southampton—for they had

become his friends during the short time of his stay amongst them—wished to give him as cordial a farewell as the welcome had been splendid; they were assembled at the railway terminus, and we were greeted with deafening cheers. Mr. Andrews was here, the frank and open-hearted Mayor of Southampton, a "self-made" man, and a living evidence that, even in the Old World, honest industry can raise an enterprising character from the rank of a daily labourer to a highly-respected public and political station. He was accompanied by Mr. Deacon, the accomplished townclerk, who knows how to enjoy wisely what he has earned honorably. After an elegant luncheon in the house of the Consul of the United States, Mr. Rodney Croskey, an American gentleman, whose acute Yankee judiciousness, matured by long European experience, make him fit for a far more important station in the service of his country, we went to the pier, followed by thousands of the people who had turned out with flying banners to catch a glimpse of the Hungarian chief. They pressed around us to shake his hands once more, and when we reached the Jupiter, the splendid steam-boat of the Peninsular and Oriental Company, they bade us farewell, with three times three, whilst the Jupiter hoisted the Hungarian colours, greeted by a royal salute from the guns of Southampton. The Jupiter went slowly down the Southampton Waters towards Cowes, there to meet the Humboldt, which was to carry us to the United States. A farewell banquet followed in the saloon, and speeches were made, toasts drunk, and cheers uttered, whilst the band on deck played polkas and waltzes, and dancing went on until dusk, when our Southampton friends took leave. A second steamer carried us to Cowes: it was night when we reached the port, but the Humboldt was not yet in sight. A little tired by the entertainment, we rested for a while in an hotel, accompanied by Lord Dudley Stuart, the friend of the oppressed, the advocate of the balance of power,—a theory which is still recognised necessary for the maintenance of peace by every English statesman, but when infringed, is never maintained by any one of them. Our rest did not last long, as it had transpired that Kossuth was in the town, and a crowd surrounded the hotel with loud cheers. The report of a gun announced now the approach of the Humboldt, which soon appeared in the darkness like a fire-vomiting dragon. Some minutes more, and we were on board.

The Humboldt is an excellent specimen of those floating palaces, which make the communication with America so easy and comfortable, that materially the Atlantic has become a safe highroad between the two great countries, whilst, morally, the interests of both have grown indissoluble. A mere fortnight's trip carries you to the United States, a country whose institutions are based on principles altogether different from those which we are accustomed to see operating in the Old World: you do not spend more time for this excursion than the Pythagorases and Lycurguses,

the Solons and Herodotuses, when they sailed from
new Greece to ancient Egypt. Greece then, not yet
embellished by arts, developing the resources of her
unparalleled geographical position with all the vigour
and arrogance of a youth proud of his future, despised
the rigid forms of old Egypt, and the experience
gathered there for thousands of years; but her sages
seeking information, still visited the land of the
Nile, whose theocratical and monarchical spirit, and
those colossal monuments of art, pervaded by the
same spirit, remained for them an unsolved but
admired riddle. The Egyptian priest smiled at the
inquisitiveness of the Greek mind; he declared openly
to Solon, that the Greeks are really but children,—
and, infatuated by the traditionary wisdom of his
forefathers, he neglected to study the new development
of the human mind in Greece. He clung too tightly
to those ancient forms, from which the spirit was
already beginning to depart; his political independence once broken by the Persians, his refined
civilisation, and his energetical nationality was cor-
roded by the Greek and Roman genius, which could
not assimilate with the Egyptian institutions: it
perished without even giving to the world the example
of a patriotic struggle against the fate. They were
dead and mummified long before they were swept
away.—It is a lesson which old Europe should remember.

II. DISCOVERY OF AMERICA BEFORE COLUMBUS.

A winter passage to America is a most unpleasant expedition; the cold prevents you from remaining on deck, and the gales and rains, so frequent in November and December, produce very soon their natural consequence, sea-sickness, among the passengers. Of all our party there were only Mr. Lemmi, Colonel Ihasz, and myself, who did not suffer. Of course we had to comfort and to amuse our friends, though we also felt a little uneasy, and were at least not fit for any serious occupation. We spent our leisure as pleasantly as might be, in playing chess, talking politics, and musing. I examined the ship's library in the saloon, and found here Bancroft's most excellent and very popular History of North America. He has again directed our attention to the expedition of De Soto, and his discovery of the Mississippi Valley, which was not less adventurous than that of Cortes. He impartially acknowledges the merits of Marquette, La Salle, and the French Jesuits: why is it then that he neglects altogether the illustrious names of those Northmen who, long before Columbus, had settled in Greenland, and sent their trading and exploring expeditions into the present territory of the United States? The history of those early discoveries is even more interesting than the adventures of De Soto, or of La Salle; they vie in romantic interest with those of Columbus; but, whilst the name of the

great Genoese is known all over the world, Erik the
Red and his children are forgotten, even by those
who do not dare to doubt the fact of the early discovery of America by the Northmen, because they
have seen it affirmed in Humboldt's Cosmus, or Cantu's
History.

Englishmen may say that the discovery of Greenland and the Western continent by the Northmen
has left no permanent results on the world, and, alas!
we are all too apt to measure men and facts by the
ultimate result only; for an American, however, the
colonisation of Greenland, and the discovery of New
England has also a patriotic interest; and, besides,
it remains a question to be decided, whether the
traditions of the Northmen had not a considerable
influence on Columbus; in every case they strengthened his belief in the possibility of finding a Western
country, though he took it for the Eastern shore of
the Indies and China. There is also another remarkable interest attached to the track of the bold seafarers of Norway. The submarine telegraphs laid
down between the shores of England and France,
and of Scotland and Ireland, are thought by many
the precursors of a great line between Europe and
America, though to convey and lay down a wire and
cable three thousand miles long seems to be impossible. But the difficulties are greatly diminished, if
the telegraph is to be carried—as it has already been
suggested—from the Orkneys first to the Faroes,
then to Iceland, so on to Greenland, and from Cape

Farewell, across Baffin's Bay, to Labrador and the United States. In this direction the greatest distance from shore to shore would be shortened to five hundred miles. And this is precisely the line pursued by the Northmen, the easiest way to the Western continent.

One of those Norwegian adventurers, who, half pirates, half merchants, so often visited the north of England, Scotland, and Ireland, for purposes either of trade or plunder, discovered Iceland in the ninth century. Norwegian chiefs and freemen, fleeing from the oppression of King Harold Harfagar, colonised the snowy island. Erik the Red, when banished from Iceland for manslaughter, sailed farther west, and came upon Greenland, towards the end of the tenth century. Many friends accompanied and followed him thither, whilst one of them, Biarni, was carried in a south-westerly direction, towards New England; but, from his anxiety to arrive in Greenland, he did not land on the shore which he saw. Leif, the son of Erik, immediately perceived the importance of the new discovery, fitted out an expedition, and proceeded first to Newfoundland, then to Nova Scotia, and, at last, to the coasts of New England. He remained there during winter, and returned with a cargo of grapes and timber. For seafarers, in a woodless country, this latter was of invaluable importance, and, therefore, several members of Leif's family explored successively the newly-discovered countries, especially Markland, the country of wood (Nova Scotia), and Vinland, the wine land (New England), in order to settle upon them. But the hostility of the aborigines, and the difficulties of the passage—several ships having been carried away by storms into the ocean—impeded their lasting colonisation of the Western continent. Separated by a dangerous sea from the mainland, Greenland could not become for America, what the Highland of Tartary had been for Asia. The new country was visited by trading parties only.

The annals of Iceland mention, as late as 1121, that Bishop Erik of Greenland sailed from thence to Vinland; the priests Adalbrand and Thorwald visited Helluland in 1285, and called it Nyja Funda Land (New Found Land); the Norwegian King Erik the Priest-hater despatched Landa-Rolf, in 1289-90, to find out this country; and, in 1347, a Greenland ship is mentioned again, which had been on a trading voyage to Markland.

The personal adventures of the early discoverers of America before Columbus are recorded at length in one of the most beautiful works of penmanship in Iceland, written between 1387 and 1395, the celebrated 'Codex Flatoiensis,' preserved now in the Royal Library at Copenhagen; and it is a well-known fact, that Columbus, in 1477, visited Iceland, where the traditions about Vinland were yet alive, though all connection with the colony of Greenland had ceased. The last bishop of Greenland was appointed in 1406. Since that time the colony has never been

heard of, though it consisted then of 280 settlements. Queen Margaret, on whom the three
Northern crowns had devolved in 1387, had made
the trade to Greenland and Iceland a royal monopoly, which could only be carried on in ships belonging to the sovereign, or licensed by him, and
certain merchants, who had visited Greenland, were
accused of treason, and only escaped punishment by
pleading that stress of weather had driven them to
those parts. Under the monopoly the Icelanders
could have no vessels, and no object for sailing to
Greenland, and the colony gradually fell into oblivion.
When, in 1721, the Norwegian clergyman, Hans
Egede, resigned his living in Norway, and obtained
permission, after many difficulties and petitions to
government, to settle as a missionary among the
Esquimaux in Greenland, he found no traces of the
missing colony; it had perished altogether. At a
later time, ruins of great churches, and tombstones
with old inscriptions, were found in different places,
but no record has been preserved mentioning the
way in which those flourishing settlements had been
broken up. Mystery hangs over their fate.

The Northmen were undoubtedly the first discoverers and first white settlers of America; but long
before them, the old Egyptians, Greeks, and Romans
had a vague tradition about a great Western country
across the ocean—the mythical Atlantis. It is not
less interesting to see that the Chinese, too, had

similar traditions about the East land, *Foo-sung*, and
that the site of America is noticed on their ancient
maps, though not as a mainland, but as a group of
large islands. The East as well as the West had a
dim presentiment of the existence of a New World,—
of a continent different from the Old one. The Irish
traditions of *Ireland the Great*, in the west; and the
Welsh chronicle of Prince Madoc, son of Owen
Gwynned, who left Wales towards the end of the
twelfth century, disgusted with her feuds, and having
discovered a fertile country in the west, put again to sea
with ten ships, and was never more heard of,—form
a new link to the evidences showing that a Western
continent was dreamt of long before Columbus.

Not only the Northmen but the Germans, too,
claim their share in the discovery of the new Continent, and vindicate the merits of their countryman,
Martin Behaim, of Nuremberg. He was a distinguished astronomer, of the school of John Regiomon-
tanus, and one of the boldest seafarers of the fifteenth
century. By introducing the use of the astrolabe, he
gave to the navigators the possibility of taking the
latitude, and ascertaining more precisely the direction
of sailing; in the service of King John the Second
of Portugal, he discovered the coasts of Congo in
Africa, and founded settlements on the Azores.
Knighted by his master, he married the daughter of
Don Job de Huerta, the governor of Fayal, where
he remained for several years. On one of his expe-

ditions, in 1483, ten years before the journey of Columbus, gales and eastern winds drove him from the Azores to the coasts of Brazils—the Prajas of Pernambuco. He thought the Southern continent a large island, and took possession of it for the crown of Portugal. Unaware of the importance of his discovery, he did not pursue it, but on the celebrated globe which he made in 1491, and which is preserved until now in the Library of Nuremberg, he recorded it, though he took the Brazils for an island belonging to the East Indies, as at this time the shores of India and China were thought to extend much farther east than they really do, and Columbus himself believed his own discovery in the Caribbean Sea to be a part of India. The great Genoese, who had come as far north as Iceland, in order to get information about the Western hemisphere, had visited also Behaim at Madeira; he became his friend, and the German seafarer communicated his maps and experience to his Italian comrade. For this reason, French, German and Portuguese historians call Behaim the discoverer of America, though Columbus, after having collected all the traditions and all the theoretical and practical evidences of the existence of a Western country, was the first who had the courage and the endurance to *seek* those shores, which others had seen by chance, and to turn them into account for himself and his master. When afterwards his name became celebrated, his detractors remembered all the ancient traditions and recent fortuitous discoveries, and found that the merits of the Genoese were but small; but Columbus did not claim a greater share of renown than really was due to him. The anecdote of the egg shows clearly that he claimed only the merit of having been the first who did intentionally what others might have done, had they had his powers of combining and his perseverance; the premises were known to everybody, he was the first to draw the conclusion. But in every case Behaim deserves to be remembered with Bartholomew Diaz and Vasco de Gama, with Columbus and Magellan, with Cabot and Cabral. He was the first who, in the Pyrenean Peninsula, diffused the knowledge about the real spherical form of the earth, who by improvements in taking the latitude, made long navigations possible across the ocean, and who by his own expeditions, showed to the bold adventurers how much they may risk, and how much there remains to discover.

III. THE AMERICANS IN EUROPE.

The passengers on board of the Humboldt presented a most varied assembly. The majority were Americans returning home; there was besides a Mexican Commodore, who had lost his left arm in one of the battles of the Republic, I think before Vera Cruz; an old German resident of Havanna, who had become a thorough Cuban, losing his temper regularly as often as the expedition of Lopez was mentioned, severa'

Frenchmen engaged in business, several German emigrants, and Lola Montes.

Though sea-sickness prevailed almost all the time of the passage, principally amongst the ladies, and the social intercourse was very limited, yet I had leisure and occasion to begin my studies of American character. I found amongst my fellow-passengers a very intelligent, sharp merchant from western New York, well acquainted with European and American politics, who, at my request, endeavoured to explain to me the dovetailed state of parties in the United States, which I was shortly to witness myself. He was a sound American patriot, but the strong party feeling, which characterises his countrymen in the States, was somewhat smoothed down by a longer residence in Europe. His stay in the old country had evidently had its good effect upon him. He was proud of being a republican, as all Americans are; but as he was a merchant who had visited Europe on business, he had no cravings to be introduced to the courts of the continent, and to the fashionable circles of the West End : he had therefore no reason to atone for his native republicanism by servile admiration of despotism abroad, and by the fashionable abuse of every republican feeling on the continent of Europe.

It is certainly striking, though easy to explain, that the majority of Americans who cross the Atlantic make themselves prominent in Europe by advocating oppression and absolutism, and abominating everything analogous to their own institutions. Of course

they are not fair specimens of the American character, and it would be very unjust to judge the
citizens of the United States by the great bulk of
the samples coming to Europe. Those who travel
for pleasure are nearly all inhabitants of the large
commercial cities, and of the sea coast States, more
or less connected by business with the conservative
Stock Exchanges of London and Paris. With the
natural inquisitiveness of their country, they wish to
see in Europe such things as they cannot see in
America. The taste for fine arts is not yet enough
developed in the States, to give those tourists a lasting pleasure in the galleries and museums of the Old
World; and besides, their time is always too much
limited to enjoy the works of art as we do; a cursory
view of the monuments being always tiresome, even
for those who have learnt how to see them. The
intercourse with the people, the study of the working
of European institutions on the masses, requires yet
more leisure, and a more philosophical and serious
turn of mind than suits with a short pleasure trip,
even for those who are ardent politicians in America,
but who have left their country for relaxation, and to
get rid for a time of politics. But one source for
gathering information is always open to them, and
it has irresistible charms for every American on
account of its novelty—this is, European society. To
be introduced to a lord, to be invited to a ball at the
Tuileries, to be presented at a court, should it be
even the court of Prince Reuss Schleiz, or Lippe

Detmold,—no matter, it is an attraction greater yet for a travelling Yankee than even for an English correspondent of 'The Times.' To obtain this aim, he gives up, not only his open democratic frankness, but even his republican pride. Fitted out by the first Parisian tailor, studying easy manners at the Jardin Mabille, learning continental politics from the weathercocks of the 'Party of Order,' and the 'Journal des Debats,' he creeps into society, flattering the principles of violence and oppression; unaware that the same society would have admitted him with more regard, had he come as an upright republican, who does not obtrude his principles of liberty, but whose demeanour itself is a living evidence of the soundness of American institutions.

We have seen American travellers at the Sorbonne, hastening to the professor's chair, in order to shake hands with Michel Chevalier, amidst the hisses of the French audience, when this ex-Saint Simonist and ex-councillor of state called the February revolution, and the establishment of a republic in France, a disastrous event; and we have heard others admiring the Russian institutions for the preservation of order and security, because the driver of the tourist was flogged without any inquest and trial by a government official, upon the simple statement of the American gentleman, that his carriage was upset by the carelessness of the driver; but, on the other side, we have occasionally made the acquaintance of several Americans in Europe who did not belong to this class. I cannot refrain from mentioning here an anecdote, which shows how republican pride can be combined with courtesy. An American traveller, in St. Petersburgh, went out on foot in March, when the snow was melting after a sudden rain. The streets presented the aspect of extensive puddles, separated at the crossings by a ridge of more solid snow, over which the foot passengers worked their toilsome way. The American was just in the midst of such a snowbridge, when he suddenly recognised the Grand Duke Constantine, in plain clothes, followed by his aide-de-camp, coming from the opposite side. The foot-path between the two puddles was not broad enough to let two persons pass by, and Mr. * * * did not wish either to turn his back uncourteously to the prince by returning from whence he came, nor to step servilely into the water; he therefore, pulling out his purse, presented it to the Grand Duke, and asked: "Odd or even?" "Even," answered the astonished prince; "You are right, Imperial Highness, I have lost, and must give way," said the American, and stept into the water. The prince was highly pleased by this proceeding, and the American received on the next day an invitation to dine with the Emperor.

IV. ESCAPE OF MADAME KOSSUTH.

(*From Mrs. Pulszky's Diary.*)

To shorten the tedious time of the passage we often went to Kossuth's cabin, and spoke of our adventures since we had lost sight of one another. He stretched himself on the upper berth, Madame Kossuth lay on the sofa, both suffering much from the sea; we sat on the floor, and, in the remembrance of bygone times, we endeavoured to make them forget the discomforts of the present. Kossuth and my husband then occasionally left us, to play at chess in the saloon, or to smoke a cigar on deck, but Madame Kossuth was unable to rise; I remained with her, and our hopes and past toils were the topic of our conversation. We had much to tell one another, for in London, in the whirl of excitement, we had scarcely found leisure for a quiet talk. I requested her to relate to us the story of her escape through Hungary. I knew only that she had been for months in the country without being discovered, yet unable to join her children, who soon were found out, and thrown into prison. I endeavoured to retain all the details in my memory, and I give her words now from recollection, with slight alterations, still necessary, that the friends who assisted her may not be exposed to the annoyances of the Austrian police, or perhaps to more fatal consequences.

"The last days in Arad," she said, "were harassing for me beyond description. Dembinski, with the faithful army, had gone towards Temesvár, instead of proceeding to Arad; Görgey, our personal enemy, had arrived in his stead. The brilliant army of the Upper Danube,—the victors of Isaszeg, who had sung patriotic hymns whilst they stormed the walls of Buda, were disorganised and dispirited. Görgey, and his former brother officers of the Austrian army, had done their work admirably, decrying the civil government, incessantly exposing the best battalions without support to the attack of the enemy, and sending away those officers who faithfully obeyed the orders of the government.

"The enemy drew nearer. On the 10th of August the order was given to attack him. I heard every cannon-shot during three painful hours. How I rejoiced when the reports grew fainter!—a sign that we were advancing; but again they got stronger and stronger; General Nagy-Sándor was evidently repulsed; and now again, as formerly at Debreczin, Görgey had not supported him. Ministerial councils were held late in the evening; Görgey came and remained for a long time closeted with my husband. A vague report spread that a pitched battle had been fought at Temesvár. It was said that our troops were advancing there, whilst in our immediate neighbourhood the enemy approached the fortress. The ministers who went to the council seemed downcast; Görgey sullen and reserved as ever. At midnight Lajos* retired to the bed-room quite exhausted. I

* Lajos is the Hungarian form for *Louis.*

let us perish together,' snatched him from the cart,
and pressed him violently to her bosom. Whilst she
was quite lost in her despair, the officer drove off.
Whereto we did not know: to get away was our
only aim. We went on, till late in the evening,
with tired horses, we reached a lonely inn; but we were
not admitted there: terror and distrust were spread
everywhere. The officer had to threaten the innkeeper with violence, if he refused to give shelter to a
dying woman, who was fleeing from the Wallacks,
before the door was opened. They carried me to the
room, and put me on the bed. The innkeeper's family
was rough and sullen, and stared stupidly at us: they
did not like us as guests. A few hours had scarcely
elapsed, when again an alarm was given that the
Wallacks were approaching. The publican began to
pack up his furniture, and drew the bed-cloth from
under me, in order to hide it, and left me on the
bare straw. My glance fell on the opposite wall, and
the well-known portrait of my husband, with his
mild countenance, looked down upon me. I remembered the time when this lithography had been made;
and when I contrasted it with my wretched condition,
a laughter cramp seized me. Ellen and the officer
carried me to the cart; I was unable to walk.

" We drove on, but every place and every inn were
filled with Austrian and Russian soldiers; there was
no safety anywhere. At last we stopped in a village,
for I could not be conveyed further. The officer knew
that a poor surgeon lived here, and he drove straight

to his house. It was a mere thatched peasant house;
the study in front, the bedroom in the rear, separated
by the kitchen. Without further asking, the officer
lifted me from the cart, carried me to the bed-room,
and put me on the bed of the surgeon, who was engaged in his study with some patients, unaware of
what was going on in the other part of his abode.
Four wooden chairs, a rickety table, and a poor bed,
were his only furniture. I was scarcely on the bed
when the surgeon entered, and to his astonishment
and dismay, found us established in his room. Surprised and impatient, he exclaimed, 'How did you
dare to put this woman on my bed? she is dying!'
But the officer calmly and sternly replied, 'If you
touch a hair of this lady, you are a dead man. She
is my sister-in-law, fleeing from the Wallacks.' The
surgeon was struck, and surmised that the company
might be different from what it appeared. He sat
down by the bed; I was delirious. Hearing the
words I uttered, he exclaimed, 'Who can this lady
be?' Ellen, fearing he might find it out himself,
said, 'She is the wife of one of the ministers, who
is now trying to escape the Austrians.' 'If only the
Governor is safe!' replied he, 'They say he is in
Turkey; where is his wife? orders are given to seize
her and her children,' and he went on deploring our
fate. I did not hear all this; Ellen told it to me
afterwards, when, under the care of the good surgeon,
I began to recover. He treated me with the utmost
attention. Ellen thanked him often, and told him

that we were not so poor as we looked, and would remunerate him with pleasure. But he declined any fee; he said he was a poor man, but a lady in such circumstances had likely more need of her money than he.

"In a few days, my host from * * * arrived, to take me back to his country-seat, as the alarm of the Wallack invasion had proved without foundation. The country was quiet; the savage hordes had been repulsed by the Russians, who no longer needed such allies.

"When Mr. * * * saw the state of my health, he thought it impossible to remove me; but once more I roused my energies, and overcame the feebleness of my frame. I rose, and in the evening I was ready to start. The surgeon entreated me not to leave yet, but to stay some days longer; but I expected tidings from my husband, my children, and my mother-in-law, so I could not remain. The poor surgeon shed tears when we left, and blessed me; he refused all remuneration. I had to put the fee, without his knowledge, into the book which lay on his table.

"My host himself drove the open carriage, in which he had come to take us. The rain poured in torrents all the night until morning, when we arrived at the castle, drenched to the skin, and I again felt very ill. I was confined to my bed, but my chamber was near enough to the drawing-room to allow me, occasionally, to hear the conversation. The third day after my arrival, a gentleman came and related, amongst other news, that Kossuth's children had been found out by the Austrians, and had been imprisoned on the very day of St. Louis. ' Kossuth's mother and sister are also imprisoned,' continued he. He spoke so loud that I heard every word. I could not suppress a scream; but, fortunately, the visitor was so deeply immersed in conversation, that he did not hear it. It was a dreadful moment. No tidings from Lajos, and of the children, such terrible news! My kind hostess had noticed my distressing cry,—she endeavoured, in vain, to comfort me. Soon afterwards another guest arrived,—not one of the patriots,—yet he related with disgust, that the Austrian General, Schlick, had issued a proclamation, threatening everybody, who should give shelter to the wife of Kossuth, with confiscation of goods, and trial by court-martial. These words, too, reached my ears, and I heard, likewise, that a price of 20,000 florins was put on my head. I was determined not to endanger my friends any longer, and when they came to my room, I declared that I felt strong enough to proceed farther. They requested me to remain, but I could not accept their self-sacrificing generosity; I did not listen to their entreaties, or to their remonstrance, that my health could not stand the fatigue of a long journey. At last they yielded to my firm resolution, and I drove away, with Ellen, to the house of a lady with whom I was acquainted. When I arrived, she told me that this part of the country was unsafe, and that but a few days before a superior officer had been arrested in the neighbourhood.

But she offered herself to accompany me to her brother-in-law. We set out; again we found every inn
crowded by Austrian soldiers; we could not venture
to go in, but remained in the carriage. Our horses
were fed in a by-street, close to the house of the
parson, who noticed us, and came out and offered us
a plate of soup. He enquired for news, whether we
had not heard anything about the Governor. 'I every
day pray for his safety,' said he; 'Oh! that his wife
were only with him! what will be her fate if they
catch her? they treat his children cruelly.' I began
to weep. He kindly asked what ailed me? I answered
that I had known the family.

"Having taken some soup, we drove on. In the
evening we arrived at my companion's brother-in-law,
a rough country-gentleman, who was first angry with
Mrs. * * * for bringing unknown persons as guests,
in such critical times. But when he saw me, he
immediately gave orders to provide for my accommodation. He sent every thing we required to our room;
yet he studiously avoided us. He probably had recognised me. I saw that my presence frightened
every one who knew me. Next morning, therefore,
I requested Mrs. * * * not to accompany me any
farther. I would not constantly expose my friends to
danger. I was unwilling to go too far from * * *
whereto alone Lajos could send me tidings; I therefore
made up my mind to travel with Ellen, assuming the
part as having been of late hospital nurses, sisters of
a Honvéd officer. My intention was, to avoid the

country-seats of those whom I personally knew, and
to live amongst the peasantry. And so we did; we
found a home amongst the lowly. Miss Mary and
her sister, the hospital nurses, were well received by
the peasants, and were safe in the cottages of the poor.
But, on the other hand, the difficulty increased, to get
reliable information about anything going on at home
and abroad.

"Often, when we stayed in a village, the peasant
women came and said to me, 'My dove, you surely are
ill; let me cook some soup for you. You look so pale!'
And when they heard that I was the sister of a Honvéd
officer, they asked me whether I knew nothing of their
master, Kossuth,—God bless him! they had hidden
his bank notes, they knew they would be of value
again. Such scenes comforted me.

"Once we arrived in one of the large Hungarian
villages on a market-day. Peasants from all parts of
the country were there, to sell their produce. But
the general talk amongst them was, less of the prices,
than about Kossuth,—Where he is?—and that he
was coming back with a Turkish army,—that he was
treated by the Turks, with all the honors due to a
sovereign,—and that he has become the ally of the
Sultan. They did not hesitate freely to utter his
name, proscribed in the castles of the gentry by
distrust, and fear of the Austrian police.

"When going to * * * I was very nearly recognized.
Sitting on a peasant-cart with Ellen, drawn by two
jades, clad in a cotton dress, my head wrapt up

in a blue handkerchief, I little thought that my appearance could rouse suspicion. It was not far from the fortress of Arad, a regiment of cuirassiers came along the road; and we had to stop whilst they passed. A gentleman of the neighbourhood, late of the Austrian army, who had married a Hungarian heiress, was cantering up the way, to meet his former brother-officers. He passed our cart, without noticing us; but when with the gay company of the Austrians he again approached us, one of them pointed to me. He rode up close to us, and stared in my face. I assumed as stupid a countenance as ever I could, and, as he turned his horse, I heard him say, 'peasant-women; nothing else.' Arrived in the neighbouring place, I sent to Arad for news, how the prisoners were treated? where Lajos was? I got the answer, that my two sons were handed over to the Jesuits, my daughter to the nuns;* that the generals were under trial by court-martial; that Austria and Russia insisted on the extradition of the refugees in Turkey; that the Sultan was undecided what course to pursue, and kept them in prison. But all these were vague rumours; nobody knew how far they could be trusted.

"I saw that I was not safe here, and therefore I took a northerly direction. But wherever I came, I found Austrian soldiers billeted in the houses of the peasants. We arrived at * * *, a large village. Night was approaching; the horses were tired; it was cold; I

* This proved untrue; they were in prison at Presburg.

could not obtain any shelter, and I began to weep.
A peasant saw it, and asked what ailed me?

" ' I do not know where to go for this night.'

" ' I would take you to my house, but it is too
far. I pity you very much' said the peasant; 'but the
upholsterer here has a spare room; it is not yet
entirely arranged, yet it is better than nothing.'

"We accepted the advice; and we found the
upholsterer and his wife such a kind-hearted, in-
dustrious, though very poor couple, that I immediately determined to stay with them. When we
told them that we wished to hire their spare room,
and to remain in their house some time, and had
concluded the bargain, they offered us food gra-
tuitously, thinking that we must be badly off to hire
such a wretched room. Not to rouse their suspicion,
I promised them a very trifling remuneration, saying,
that we had money left. But I did not dare to buy
better furniture for my room; I only requested them
to get us, if possible, a Vienna newspaper in the
village; 'because,' said I, 'I have a brother with the
refugees in Turkey, and I would like to know what
has become of them all.' In a few days they brought
me the 'Ostdeutsche Post,' but not of the last date.
I hastily glanced over it, and read in the correspondence from Widdin, that the refugee-question
was settled; they were to be given up; and the
Austrian General, Haustab, had already gone to escort
them back. I became nearly mad, and wrote to my
friends in * * * that if the prisoners were coming,

they should send me notice without delay, that I
might join my husband to die with him. My poor
hostess saw my distress, and, full of commiseration,
said that she never again would get me a newspaper,
as it was very bad for me. Yet at the same time
rumours were afloat, that the Sultan had refused to
give up the Hungarians, and so I remained in an
agony of fear and hope for a whole week. It was
the most painful time of my life.

"I again got papers; I looked first for the news from
Turkey, and it tranquillized me a little; but when I
glanced at the correspondence from Pesth, I saw that
Count Louis Batthyàny had been executed. I swooned
when I read this. It then struck my hosts that I
might perhaps be Countess Batthyàny; and from
this day they made a fire in my stove, though they
denied themselves this luxury.*

"On the next market-day, knowing how poor they
were, I sent Ellen to buy three cart-loads of straw.
When they were brought to the upholsterer, he came
to me and asked who had bought it? I said, ' I
had done it.' 'Goodness me!' he exclaimed, 'are
you so rich, Miss Mary, that you can spare so much
money?' When he had left me, I heard him talk
with his wife, that I must be a great lady; and they
no longer allowed their journeymen to go into the
kitchen when I was there.

* In the treeless plains of Lower Hungary wood is expensive. The
poorer classes burn straw; but even this is not cheap, on account of
the great masses required to produce a comfortable fire. It is to be
observed, that usually the winter is here mild.

"In the evening my landlord and his wife used to come to my room for a talk. He smoked his short pipe, and enquired if I did not know 'where their good *master* Kossuth was?' 'Had he only never trusted to a gentleman,'—said he—'had he only thrown himself entirely on the people,—we would have stood by him till the last! Had he only left his children with a peasant, they would not be in prison; but the gentry have betrayed him and his children!"

"Forgetting where I was, I said, 'really the people are good, and have noble hearts. If I succeed to get away, and God afterwards bring us back again, I will richly return your kindness, and I will furnish your whole house.' The pipe dropt from the mouth of my host, and his wife rose and exclaimed 'Dear me! who is it before whom I stand? Miss Mary!—it is impossible that you should be Miss Mary!'

"I saw my mistake, and told them that my brother had, in the last event, rendered great service to Kossuth, who surely would do everything for him.

"After this day they did not quite believe me. They treated me with much more respect, and their journeymen made me a present of a footstool. Soon after I saw by the papers that there was no longer any danger that Lajos should be given up: they even said, that he was on his way to London. But I had as yet no letter from him, and no tidings from my children.

"My kind friend from * * * visited me and said, 'that he had heard a gentleman had arrived from

Widdin with letters for me, and that on the morrow, he would be at the country seat of Mr. * * *.' I immediately ordered a cart to proceed thither. My friend cautioned me not to go, as this might be an Austrian trap, and the gentleman from Widdin an Austrian spy. But I was determined to risk anything to obtain certain information.

" The weather was so bad, that I had great difficulty to get a driver. I paid my lodgings, took leave of my good hosts; told them that, in case I did not return, they should keep the things left in my room as remembrance, and I went.

" The driver was in bad humour. He grumbled what a folly it was to travel in such weather! and then he cursed the Austrians for the new taxes, and began to talk politics. He said to me, ' we will not obey the king; for he is no king; he is only a German Emperor: He has no right to command in Hungary. He is not even crowned, and therefore he is a usurper.'

" ' But, Sir,' said I—' if they find the crown, and crown him regularly, what will you do then?' He paused a moment. 'Then the lightning of heaven shall strike him: we won't obey him:' he angrily replied.

" When I arrived at the village, I sent Ellen to the castle to say, that I was waiting in the hotel. The gentleman of the manor came hastily in great confusion to me and said, that he had not admitted the messenger from Widdin; for he distrusted him. He reproached me that I ventured to come to a place, strongly watched by the Austrians: he asked whether I required money, and entreated me to depart immediately. In fact, Austrians were at his table, and he could not stay one moment longer without rousing suspicions, equally fatal to me and to him.

" I wept that my hopes were again defeated; for I had made up my mind to proceed with the messenger to Widdin; I had to return again to the kind upholsterer.

"My great object was now to send money and tidings to Lajos, because the Austrian papers stated, that he had been robbed in Turkey of all he possessed, and that the refugees there were starving and illtreated. I knew, moreover, that there was a report spread, perhaps by my own friends, in order to deceive the Austrian police, that I was dead. I did not wish that such tidings should reach Widdin, and I, therefore, was willing, in case the papers would mention it, to declare, through the press, that I was alive. But how to convey a letter to my husband? To get to him myself, seemed now impossible; I had no chance of obtaining a passport under an assumed name; for my friends would not venture such an application; they were paralysed by fear. I looked for assistance to another quarter.

" I had learnt from Ellen, that the son of the schoolmaster, an educated young man, had become an apprentice at our upholsterer's; I sent for him. He came up stairs whistling, and his cap on his head;

he opened my door, but when he beheld me, he turned pale and trembled. He had seen me formerly in Pesth, but had little thought that Miss Mary and I were the same person. He asked for my commands.

"I told him, that I wished to send him with a letter to Widdin. He answered, that he could not do it without the consent of his parents; his brother had fallen in battle, and he had promised his bereaved mother, not to go into any dangerous enterprize without her knowledge, but he did hope that she would not deny her consent. Next day he returned, blushing, and declared that he must decline my commission. His mother had knelt down before him, and entreated him to keep clear from politics. For her sake he had given up the career of learning, and had turned upholsterer; he could not resist her wishes, and felt ashamed that he could not serve me. I did not utter a single word, but I was in despair. I had to wait again.

"One evening we heard heavy steps in the street, a detachment of soldiers was coming, and stopt before the house. Ellen entreated me to flee, as they surely were sent to seize me, but I was too tired to attempt anything for my safety. I said, apathetically ' go down and open the door; I do not conceal myself.' She went, but in a few moments she returned, laughing. It was a mistake. The soldiers were not seeking me. In the dark, they had taken the house of the upholsterer for the town-house.

"A couple of days after this adventure, there was

again a great alarm. In the evening two persons knocked violently at the door, and said aloud, in German, so that I should hear it, 'Does Miss Mary live here? we have a message for her from Turkey.' I rushed to the door, pushing aside the upholsterer, who would not admit them; a lady and gentleman entered, and handed me a letter; it was the hand-writing of Lajos. My emotion was so sudden that I could not read, I sobbed violently. I was soon apprized that Lajos was to be detained somewhere in Asia, and I declared that I was ready to follow my new friends to join him. Madame W * * * and Mr. M * * *, who had come from Widdin to take me to Turkey, were utterly unknown to me, and they asked me whether I trusted them, and did not suspect it was the Austrians who had sent them. 'And had all the despots of the world sent you,' answered I, 'you bring me this letter, and I follow you.' I now first learned that another letter had previously arrived, but my friends had burnt it, that it might not induce me to attempt an escape over the nearest Turkish frontier, where the Austrians were keeping strict watch. It was with the greatest unwillingness that they had revealed my hiding-place to the messengers of my husband, so general was their suspicion. Mrs. W * * * told me we had no time to lose; she had a passport for Pesth, and as the last steam-boat was to go thence in a few days down the Danube, if we did not reach Pesth in time the difficulties would become incalculable. I immediately prepared for departure, and next morning, the first of December, we started in a light open carriage for the railway. A snow-storm had beat upon us all the way, and my face became sore from the frost.

"At Szolnok we took seats in a third-class carriage, trembling lest some passenger should recognise me in my disguise. It was the same railway by which we had left Pesth when Windischgrätz was coming, and on which we had returned in triumph from Debreczin!

"We were surrounded by danger. Several Jews, who happened to sit near us, mentioned the name of my husband, and spoke about me; in the first-class carriage I remarked, at the stoppages, several ladies whom I knew. When we arrived at the railway terminus in Pesth, a great crowd was waiting for the train; I held my handkerchief before my face, and Mr. M * * * requested the policeman, to whom he had handed my passport, not to delay us long, as I had violent tooth-ache. The policeman let us pass; we took a cab, and drove across the Danube to the lodgings of Mrs. W * * *, which she had kept ever since she had set out in search of me, upon her arrival from Turkey. It was a small house; the landlady was cooking in the kitchen, through which we had to go to the room. 'Good morning,' she said to Mrs. W * * *, when we arrived, and when she saw me she turned red, and began to weep, but did not say a word.

"The wife of a tailor, across the street, had also recognized me. She told Mrs. W * * * that her

late brother had appeared to her in a dream, saying,
that the lady of the Governor was at Buda, and that
everybody would be punished severely who should
betray her; and that she believed in the vision, as her
brother had been a pious priest. Mrs. * * * gave
her ten florins, with the advice to have a mass read
for the repose of her brother, that his soul might not
haunt her sleep; and she also reminded her, that in
these hard times it was very dangerous to have such
dreams.

"Through the kindness and exertions of Mrs. W.,
I got further opportunity to send a letter to the prison
of my children. But, in the meantime, winter set in,
suddenly. The Danube froze; no steamer could leave
Pesth, and we had to go by land, where annoyances
and dangers with passports and visitations were unavoidable. With the greatest difficulty I got a passport
under an assumed name; my friends were indefatigable, and had left no means untried to get it. At
last they succeeded. When we started, our landlady
kissed my hand, and said, ' God the Almighty bring
you back !' Everywhere on the Theiss, and on the
Danube, I found the same feeling amongst the many.

"Through snow and cold, we reached the fortress
of Peterwardein, after a tedious journey. We again
found the hotel overcrowded, and were shown to the
ball-room,—the only place unoccupied. It was a large
hall, dimly lighted by the tallow candle which the
waiter put on the table. The door was not locked,
and people occasionally peeped in. I recognized

amongst them Count * * *, an Austrian partizan. He
seemed to suspect something wrong, and entered the
room. Fearing to be recognized, I again complained
of violent toothache to M * * *, hiding my face with
my handkerchief; and my companions inquired of the
Count, whether he did not know a dentist in the town,
and began to overwhelm him with so many questions,
that he was annoyed, and withdrew.

"The next morning we proceeded farther; but
scarcely were we fifteen miles on our way, when some
soldiers came up to our carriage and stopt it, 'We have
orders to escort you to the nearest magistrate,' said
the sergeant; 'you have to give up your passports.'
'Why?' asked M * * *; 'Because you are denounced
as travelling under assumed names.' It was a very
disagreeable moment, but no choice was left. We
arrived in a small borough, and were escorted to the
town-house. The sergeant went into the court-hall.
We had to wait in the ante-room, but in a very few
minutes were summoned before the magistrate. He
stood at his desk, in a dignified manner,—a stout, jolly,
red-faced German gentleman—with our passports in
his hand, and in a solemn way he said :—

"'Ladies and gentlemen, you are accused of travelling under assumed names. This is a serious charge,
and I must immediately enter upon the inquest. You
had better confess your misdemeanour, as I shall
easily ascertain the fact.' After this preamble he
turned towards me, and inquired, putting a pair of
spectacles on his nose, 'What is your name?'

" ' Mary Smith,' I said boldly, with a light curtsey.

" ' Mary Smith !' he repeated emphatically, and looked into the passport. ' Mary Smith ! why, this is really the name of the passport. Where from ?'

" ' From Pesth.'

" ' Where to ?'

" ' To Semlin.'

" ' For what purpose ?'

" ' To visit friends.'

" After every one of my answers, he again looked into the passport, and said, rather astonished, ' But everything is correct.'

" After Mrs. W * * * and Mr. M * * * had gone through the same process, the magistrate turned to the sergeant, and sternly reproached him for having dared to interfere with peaceable travellers, whose passports were entirely regular. He turned then towards us, and dismissed us with an apology that he had detained us. The sergeant grumbled and mumbled something about his orders; we bowed and withdrew.

" We soon arrived at Semlin. Across the Danube there lay Belgrád—for us the place of safety; but the difficulty of crossing was increased so much the more by the quarantine regulations, as our passports were good only for Semlin, and not farther.

" M * * *, who travelled in the character of a paper-manufacturer, went to the police-office, and requested the gentlemen there, to grant him permission to visit Belgrád, as he had some business to transact with the printer of the government paper. After some delay the permission was given. M * * * went away, but here returned again to the officer, and said that his sister, and her friend, who travelled with her, would worry him much if he did not take them to the Turkish fortress. They wished very much to buy samples of the celebrated Turkish dried prunes on the spot. It was an affair but of a few hours; they would leave all their luggage at the office, as they were only going just to take a peep at the Turks. *

" His eloquence carried his object. A quarantine-officer, was sent with us to the river, to keep an eye upon us; and in high spirits we hired a boat, to carry us over to Serbia. But when we put off the Hungarian bank, deep emotion overcame me; it was my country that I was leaving, perhaps for a long time; and I wept.

" ' What is the matter?' asked the quarantine-officer. 'She is frightened on the water,' said Mrs. W * * *, 'might we not founder here?' 'Nonsense!' answered he; and laughed at my cowardice.

"At Belgrád M * * * stopt at the first public house, and invited the quarantine-man to take a glass of wine with him; for he felt quite chilly, and the ladies also were hungry. As there was no difficulty to persuade the Austrian, we went in and ordered

---

* The *city* of Belgrád is Serbian, the *fortress* Turkish. Serbia is a separate principality, but pays tribute to the Sultan. These Serbs must not be confounded with those of Hungary.

breakfast. The two gentlemen began to drink; Mrs. W * * * remarked, after a little time, that while they were emptying the bottle, and the breakfast getting ready, we would go across the street to buy shoes. ' Don't stay long,' said M * * *; ' we shall return in a minute ' was the answer : but, once in the street, we hastened to the British Consulate,—and I was safe.

" Mr. Fonblanque, the British Consul, was not in town ; but we found out the Sardinian Consul, who congratulated me on my escape. M * * * soon joined us; he had left his companion at the bottle. Shortly after, Mr. Fonblanque arrived, and showed me great kindness during my stay in Serbia.

" I sent a message to the Serb minister, that I expected, from the chivalrous character of his nation, that they would grant me protection, and the orders necessary for travellers, who pass through a country without high-roads, where no conveyance can be found, but by special order of government. The minister was surprised, but soon promised and offered every assistance. I was invited to a country-seat of the prince, to remain there until spring; for, they said, the roads were impracticable in winter; nobody could travel otherwise than on horseback. A winter journey by carriage was unheard of, and in an open sledge it would be dangerous to my health.

" I was detained in this way for a whole week, and I began to fear that I should not be allowed to proceed to my husband. When I complained of the delay, I was requested to state precisely what I wanted. I replied, ' Nothing, but to be able to join my husband; and if no orders are given to this end, I must consider myself a prisoner, and I will escape, when I can.'

" The aide-de-camp of the Prince came now to me, and told me he would be happy to accompany me on my journey, if I had made up my mind for many toils and difficulties, as a winter journey was unusual for ladies in these parts; but when I refused to stay longer in Serbia as their guest, he begged to be excused, if he could not afford me all the comforts he wished. He handed me a letter of protection from the prince, and said that orders were given along our whole road to receive the lady, escorted by him, as the guest of the prince.

" We set out; the cold was intense, the roads dreadful; the snow impeded our progress; often we heard the howl of wolves in the evening; the sledge was upset; sometimes we could not get horses, and had to go forward with oxen. Occasionally we had to sleep in a stable; as I would not go into the under-ground, unclean, unventilated huts of the peasants. At other times, we found a comfortable shelter in the houses of the lord lieutenants of the counties and the government officials.

" The orders of the prince had roused considerable curiosity along our road; people could not guess who the mysterious lady was, travelling with an English passport, in winter, as the guest of the prince.

" When we arrived at places where accommodation
could be found, the gentleman of the manor received
us at the gate, in his picturesque national costume.
On the threshold we found the lady in the rich Serbian
dress; she attended us at dinner in the antique way.
When we sat at table, she remained at the door; the
meals were brought by the servants to her, and she
tendered them to us with the natural dignity and
grace peculiar to the East. At night she came with
her maids, who carried the pillows, trimmed with
French lace, and the richly embroidered silk blankets,
one after the other, was handed to her; she prepared
the couch and invited me to rest.

" The aide-de-camp was often asked who I was; but
he always met the enquiries with some joke, and
evaded the answer. He seemed pleased with the
mystery which surrounded us. Once only, in the
moment of our departure, he told the lord lieutenant
of a county, who had entertained us with splendid
hospitality, that his guest was the wife of Kossuth.
He was evidently struck, and passionately exclaimed,
' Why did you not tell it me before? I would have
treated her with greater honours.'

" At Widdin, the aide-de-camp left me. He was
a most amiable, chivalrous man, who, even on the
Turkish territory, defended me against the Austrian
Consul, who, even here, in a foreign country, attempted
to annoy us by examination of passport and visitations
of luggage. He probably thought, that I carried the
crown of St. Stephen in my carpet-bag.

"From Widdin the Pasha sent me to Shumla, and after five months of dreadful separation, I was again united to my husband."

V. TURKISH HOSPITALITY.

The usual cold and rainy weather on the great bank of Newfoundland, confined us again to the state-rooms and dining-room, and the conversation with our new American acquaintances turned on the manner in which Kossuth would be received in the States. "He is the nation's guest," we were told, "and nobody except Lafayette, has ever been invited by Congress to the United States. The nation will show how she honours her guest, for there is no man living more popular in America then Kossuth." It seemed strange that the exiled chief of a nation, scarcely known before her last, though glorious but apparently unsuccessful, struggle,—a man persecuted by all the absolute powers on earth, calumniated by the most important papers of Europe, unconnected in any way with the history or interest of the United States,— should excite such an intense feeling on the Western shores of the Atlantic. Yet, after our experience in England, where the entire populations of the great manufacturing cities, turned out to give him a hearty welcome, astonishing the upper classes of society by their unusual sympathy, I did not doubt the correctness of the statement. It is an instinctive feeling with the masses, that he is the great man of the

people, who, though defeated and betrayed, has
bestowed more lasting benefits on the oppressed
classes of Eastern Europe, than any successful conqueror. Even in Turkey, where there exists hardly
any public opinion, where the horizon of the individual does not extend beyond the family and the
village or city interests, he was everywhere received
as the Padishah of Hungary, the guest of the Sultan,
in spite of all the hidden intrigues, and open threats
of Russian and Austrian diplomacy, from the Ambassadors down to the Vice-Consuls.—When he arrived
at Widdin, Zia Pasha showed him every honour, and
exerted himself to make him comfortable, requesting
him to consider himself the guest of the Sultan.
Zia was a Turk of the old school, strictly adhering
to the orders he received. The Hungarian soldiers,
who were encamped around Widdin, were badly provided with clothes, and as the weather began to be
cold, Kossuth requested the Pasha, to allow the
Hungarians to come in town and give their labour
for hire, in order to get the means for buying cloaks.
The Pasha said, "I cannot allow that the guests of
the Sultan ever should be compelled to work, in order
to provide for their wants." "Then buy cloaks for
them," answered Kossuth. "This I cannot do,"
replied Zia; "I have no orders for it." Kossuth
retired somewhat dissatisfied, but Zia had reported
the request immediately to the Divan, and in a fortnight the order from Stambul had arrived, and the
Hungarians were provided with cloaks.

In Tergova, the Pasha had prepared a great dinner for the Sultan's guest, and in order to show his regard, he for the first time in his life made use of a fork at the meal, and took even the grapes with it, wishing to accommodate himself to the customs of his guest. Kossuth, in order to return the compliment, and show how he appreciated the Pasha's courtesy, took the meal with his fingers. Both felt the delicacy of these proceedings, but of course made no remark whatever about the matter. The Pasha of Varna had even French dishes prepared for him, cooked with lard, and was present at the dinner, where the forbidden pork was served to his guest.

In Brussa, the chief of the Dervishes came to meet him, and poured water on his path, and gave him his blessing. In Kutayia, the Turkish population lined the streets on his arrival, and, crossing their hands on their breasts, bade him a respectful welcome. Soliman Bey, who had to guard him, did all he could to cover the precautions necessary to prevent escape with the greatest courtesy and attention. At his daily visit he never forgot to present a bunch of flowers to Madame Kossuth, and sugar-plums and fruits to the children. The officer who accompanied the "guests" as often as they left the barracks, carried the children, or whatever they had bought at the bazaar or shops; he was more their servant than their keeper.

Every attention was paid to the wishes of Kossuth and his family. He wished to have a garden for the

cultivation of flowers, and was immediately offered
the choice of the most convenient amongst all the
gardens of the city; and as the weather grew hot,
and he desired a small kiosk to shelter him from the
sun's rays, an elegant spacious garden-house was
built for him. When the children arrived, Soliman
welcomed them with heaps of cakes, and two ponies
for their pleasure; and if sometimes he made promises which he could not keep, he submitted meekly
to all subsequent reproaches, and said, "You are
right, I am but the poor donkey that must bear the
burden and the lashes, in order that the proud steeds
at Constantinople should appear in full glory."
When Urquhart came to Kutayia, accompanied by
Regaldi, the celebrated Italian improvisatore, and at
the dinner given by Mr. Massingberd, the strains of
his poetry, inspired by the occasion, enraptured the
company; the improvisations were translated for the
Turk, who wished to know the cause of the excitement; and having understood the enthusiasm of
Regaldi, he, too, offered a sentiment. He said,
turning to Kossuth, "There was once a golden vase
of the most beautiful form, but two rocks fell upon
it, and crushed it,—it lost its form, but still it
remained gold; whilst the shapeless rocks are but
rocks." And Regaldi had to acknowledge that the
Eastern poet had won the palm. When Madame
Wagner died, who had saved Madame Kossuth, and
brought her out from Hungary, Soliman ordered the
troops to escort the burial, and invited the Greek

priest, who otherwise is not allowed to appear publicly
in his clerical attire, to enter the barracks, where
Kossuth and the Hungarians resided; and to head
the funeral procession clad in pontificals, with the
cross raised in his hand.   Not only Kossuth and the
Hungarians, but all the Christian inhabitants of
Kutayia, were treated with more respect than formerly; for the Turks said, the Hungarian Padishah
would not like it if his co-religionists were not treated
kindly.   When in August, Soliman came at last with
the tidings that the guests of the Sultan were allowed
to depart, he was overcome by emotion, he kissed the
hands of Kossuth, and spoke: "You are free, and
now you will find friends everywhere ; pray do not
forget those who were your friends when you had
no others."   The Turks of Kutayia could not conceive why Kossuth wished so much to leave them.
"Are you not happy here?" they asked; "we like
you and respect you, and the Sultan provides for your
wants; why don't you rather remain with us than go
to strangers?"

Really the Turks have proved towards Kossuth
that they fully deserve their ancient renown for
hospitality.

Captain Lynes, of the Humboldt, exerted himself in
every way to show his kindness to our party; he did
everything to cheer up the suffering passengers, and
to afford all possible comforts, though some of the
sea-sick, and especially the ladies, grew impatient
sometimes.   People are too apt to take the short

summer-passages for the rule: a fortnight's sail from Cowes to New York seemed to us all a very bad run. It is true we had always headwinds, and encountered a series of gales; the rolling of the ship was often unpleasant, though she was very comfortably fitted, and her narrow form, which is necessary on account of the narrow entrance into the Havre docks, makes her very fast-sailing. Towards the end of our journey the weather became less ungenial, the ladies were sometimes able to take a walk on deck; the conversation became more general, and at our arrival in America, we found that, after all, the passage had been a very agreeable one.

CHAPTER II.

STATEN ISLAND, NEW YORK CITY.

I. ARRIVAL AT STATEN ISLAND.

(*From Mrs. Pulszky's Diary.*)

OUR passage was drawing to a close. It is with
a voyage as we often find it with an associate—whose
best advantages strike us most in the hour of parting; when, forgetting the annoyance he may have
caused us, we remember only the bygone pleasures
spent together. Though sadly tossed about during a
fortnight's gale, worn out almost to that state of
loathsome indifference which is characteristic of sea-
sickness, yet at the approach of the coast, we all
felt that we had grown familiar with that borderless
ocean, on which our eye had rested with longing
after the dear friends from whom we sailed, and on
which we gazed with hope and with wonder, looking
forward to the new world which was to unrol before
us. The unbounded sea has an inexpressible charm.
We all felt it, and this sympathy drew us closer
together. The last evening before touching land, we
saw more of the society on board than had been the
case during the whole of the voyage, and at dinner
the cordial feelings expressed themselves in toasts,
and were enthusiastically manifested by cheers for
Kossuth.

It was a few minutes after midnight on the 5th of
December, when a rocket was thrown from the deck
of the Humboldt, to announce our arrival in the bay
of New York, and this signal was followed by the
discharges of cannon from the ship which were instantly echoed from the shore.   The vessel continued
to fire guns from the time of her passing the Narrows
until she reached the Quarantine Ground, from
whence a salute of thirty-one guns greeted us.   The
Humboldt stopped, and Dr. Doane with Colonel
Berzenczey and the reporters of the New York press,
boarded her.   Dr. Doane proceeded to the saloon, and
addressed Kossuth in a short but very eloquent speech.
During the reply the passengers clustered together
on deck, and our excellent Captain Lynes shook
hands with us : we thanked him for his cordial hospitality and his attentive kindness, and took leave of
everybody—of our fellow-travellers and fellow-suf-
ferers, of the sailors, the black waiters and the white
chamber-maid ;   and we threw a grateful parting
glance on the safe vessel, when we descended her
slippery ladder, and jumped into the unsteady boat.
Madame Kossuth and I both screamed loud, and
felt quite glad to draw ashore, and to step, though
with wavering foot, on the steady soil.   It appeared
to us new to tread again firm land, and to see windows
of extensive houses flickering with light.   Doctor
Doane accompanied us to his own kind family circle.
Midnight was past, yet the venerable mother of our
host, his amiable wife, her sisters and her children,

and even the baby with wide-open eyes, were assembled round the fireside, tendering us the comforts of their home. Easy sofas and rocking chairs, carpets and crackling wood-fire were most acceptable after our chilly voyage; and the welcome was so warm, that we felt none of the misgivings natural to foreigners, intruding at an unusual hour into a stranger's house.

The conversation opened with questions of how we had borne the passage? and poor Madame Kossuth, how much she must have suffered with a frame so tried, and her health broken by unparalleled hardships. And all eyes turned wondering towards her pale countenance; and the cook, and the nurse, and the housemaid came to the room, and mingled their questions and their sympathy with that of their mistress.

Meanwhile Kossuth had been followed to his apartment by Major Hagedorn, with several militia officers, and addresses were delivered and answered. It was three o'clock before we retired to bed, too much worn out and excited to find rest. When at last we sank asleep, hoping not to wake before the breakfast bell rang, we were suddenly roused by a heavy cannonade. I looked at the watch, it was but half-past six. Unaccustomed, at such an hour, to so thundering an ovation, I rushed to the window looking out on the sea. The sun was rising in glorious magnificence, and lighted up the haze stretching over the waters, a broad zone of fire extended over the edge of the ocean, like a crimson band dividing the

deep blue sky from the green sea. It was so beautiful
that I felt quite glad at the peculiar hospitality of
the authorities of Staten Island, who, zealous to
honour our arrival, broke into our sleep with so early
a discharge of their guns. Yet this neglect of physical comfort, strange as it must strike every European,
seems quite natural with Americans. We Hungarians
likewise can toil and make shift in times of struggle,
but when in peace and affluence we like to enjoy
leisure. Not so here, the Americans are always in a
hurry, hardly noticing what their table offers, they
take that which happens to stand before them, and
treat their meals as a business to be dispatched as
quickly as possible. And as for sleep, they appear to
consider it rather an unlucky habit to be restrained
as much as possible. Therefore, when I peeped out
of the room, to see if others too had been aware of
the roaring salute, I saw the whole household busily
walking to and fro, on the passage and the stairs, and
the lady of the house greeted me, obviously not
astonished that I was up so early. I remarked,
" Your rest has been very short." " We did not go
to bed at all," was the reply ; " we wished to accommodate your party as well as possible, and we do not
mind at all staying up."

The morning sparkled brightly, the skies were
clear and transparent as the glance of youth ; the
small garden below was laid out in neat beds ; the
trees were newly planted ; a whitewashed *Kiosk*,
with a red top and blinds, painted grass-green, looked

quite smart; everything bore the varnish of freshness, and brought home to my mind that all around was new and young. And yet when I turned round, and beheld across the bay whole worlds of cities, spreading before my eyes, it appeared like the realization of a fairy-tale.

The housemaid entering, interrupted my meditation with the question, what she could do for me? she would be glad to do anything; and she sat down enquiring what I wanted, and assured me she would be very glad to help me. I answered that I found my wants provided for; but she continued to urge on her services with good-natured garrulity, till at last she rose, and I thought I had done with her. But after a short while she re-appeared in great finery, a mixture of a lady's winter and summer toilet, a dark silk shirt and white lace sleeves appended to a muslin jacket. It appears, that when she had found she could do nothing for my comfort, she thought she ought at least to dress, in order to please me.

Down stairs in the dining-room we found our amiable hosts, expecting us with breakfast; the children too, formed part of the company. Sturdy independent little things, with their own views and their own will. This is the feature characteristic of American children of all classes. Shyness I never met with in them; self-thought and self-management, are remarkably developed, but likewise premature self-will, an obstacle to self-control, dangerously fostering the ungovernable passions which people so many lunatic asylums in the States.

Staten Island, at the entrance of the estuary of New York, is, in summer, a favourite resort of the society of the cities around the bay, though the state of New York has established here the great fever hospital.   Contagious ship fever reigns so often on board of the crowded emigrant ships, especially when head-winds detain them for a long time at sea, and the provisions are scarce, that the health of the city was in continual danger.   No ship is therefore allowed to land at New York before it has been visited by the physician of the quarantine at Staten Island.   The heavy expenses for the great hospital are but scantily met by the dollars which the captains of the vessels pay for every arriving passenger, and which is included in the passage-money.   The burden of keeping the quarantine devolves exclusively upon the city and state of New York, the general government does not contribute to the costs of the establishment, though the emigrants usually pass as soon as possible through the state, hastening to the west.   But the American says, New York is the first sea port of the union; the principal outlet of the products of the north-west; it must therefore bear also the drawbacks and inconveniences of this prominent position.   Dr. Doane had the management of the quarantine, and told me how miserable are the thousands of Irish who weekly arrive at that hospital.   He accomplished his task as their physician with the noble devotion of a practical philanthropist, and little did I think, when he pictured to me the woes of the poor Irish people, that he himself would soon fall a prey to the fearful complaint from which he had rescued so many of them. Shortly after we left his hospitable roof, he caught the dangerous disease in the accomplishment of his duty, and died in two days, a victim of his zeal.

From breakfast we were called to the balcony, by shouts, and trumpets, and drums. The militia band of the island, followed by hundreds of hurraing people, greeted Kossuth. He came out to thank them on the balcony, which was so thronged with visitors, that we had good reason to think the frail construction would give way; therefore we, retired, probably to the disappointment of the daguerreotypists, three of whom, I understood, were busily employed to catch Kossuth's likeness, whilst he was welcomed by the crowd.

Several of our Hungarians were there, who, unable to find employment in overcrowded England, had proceeded to the United States. We found the great majority doing well; and this is not only owing to the much greater facility of getting work in America, but, in respect to those who in Hungary ranked amongst the higher classes of society, to the circumstance, that, whilst in the Old World all physical labour is considered ungentlemanlike, in America, on the contrary, not to work is looked upon as thoroughly degrading. An idle man never can meet

3 §

there with sympathy, whatever his previous position may have been; and if a man cannot work with his brains, he is expected to labour with his hands. In a country where every one who will work, can earn his livelihood, age, sickness, or vice, alone can lead to helplessness. In the States every one is respected who can help himself, whilst only those are assisted who are disabled by age or sickness.

Amongst those who came to express their joy at the arrival of the great Hungarian, I felt most interested at Kagigahgabow, the Ojibbeway chief, who, since he has adopted the ungraceful dress-coat of civilization, calls himself George Copway. He long ago had attracted my attention, as the author of the traditional history of his nation, and now I heard him deliver the following address, most touching from the lips of one torn irretrievably from his nation, because he tasted the fruit of the tree of civilisation, under whose shade he has found shelter. He spoke:

"I am very glad that I see you. I am very glad to give you my hand, and in the name of my nation and of this country, bid you welcome. Having suffered like yourself, I am here alone to represent the Indian nations of this country. I am one of those who peopled North America before the Anglo-Saxon race came hither. My home is in the West, where my nation lives. I am glad that the Anglo-Saxon race has learned the word 'Liberty.' The Indian of this country enjoyed it before him, and now it has gone back to the old country, and is now becoming

the motto of all nations;—and to-day I thank the
Great Spirit, that He has saved my life to welcome
you to our shores."

Kossuth responded to these words by a warm pressure of the hand.

In private intercourse I found Mr. Copway much
less reserved and silent than the Indians in general,
yet his olive countenance, with strongly marked,
broad cheek-bones, bears the stamp of his origin.

Our conversation was interrupted by the approach
of a procession and a file of carriages, which conveyed
us to a hill, about half a mile distant, where a large
tent was erected for a public meeting. The citizens
of Staten Island were zealous to be the first to greet
and yet more to hear Kossuth. The Hungarian
colours and the American flag gaily fluttered in the
invigorating morning breeze, the clamour was great,
the throng dense, the band played merrily, and the
guns thundered incessantly. After a little tear and
wear of our clothes, and some pressure not quite
pleasant, we were led into the tent, close to the platform raised for Kossuth. The tent was decorated
with banners, commemorating the support America
had got from foreign countries when struggling for
liberty, and the duty of the Americans to do to others
as they had done to them. Intervention for non-
intervention was the leading idea. But the audience
little seemed to notice the pageantry, their whole
attention was occupied by the hero of the day. They
were bent on every word that fell from the lips of the

soul-stirring orator, and his dignified deportment evidently impressed the crowd; it was no longer boisterous curiosity elbowing to the right and left; but the anxiety not to lose one accent, or one glimpse, established a silence and order which no police could have achieved.   Only here and there a little ragged urchin popped from some corner, making his way to the platform, and taking his stand with a most democratic determination.   In vain I strove to make one of them understand that my foot was not a stool, he persisted in using it as such, and the only concession I could obtain was, to transfer him from my right foot to the left.

After Kossuth's reply to the address of Mr. Locke, in behalf of the citizens of Staten Island, the stir of curiosity again awoke, and General Paez, the companion in arms of Bolivar, who welcomed the great Hungarian in Spanish, and the address on behalf of the German citizens of the United States were repeatedly interrupted by the pressure of the multitude, especially by ladies, who not content with hearing and seeing, were anxious to shake hands, or to carry relics home; one of them succeeded likewise in cutting a button from Kossuth's overcoat.   Great numbers of people were introduced to him, and those whom no desperate effort could carry through the circle by which he was barricaded, tried to shake hands at least with Madame Kossuth, or with some of our Hungarian gentlemen, whom they recognised by their differently shaped hats.   The sturdy melody of the Yankee Doodle was again played by the band, and closed the ceremony in the tent; and when we had fairly got out of introductions, handshakings, and squeezes, and at last were safely escorted to the carriages, the procession was resumed.

Already more familiar, and therefore less bewildered than in the morning, with the clamour and the throng which surrounded us ever since we had landed, I now surveyed the procession which unfolded before us. The different companies of the militia, the Odd Fellows in their quaint 'regalia,' the firemen's companies, the German turners (gymnastical associations), and the motley crowd presented a lively scene, as they moved on, hurraing and shouting incessantly. They seemed indefatigable, for, regardless of the biting cold, they carried us all round the island, from the hills to New Brighton, and from thence to Stapleton. All along we saw nice villas, wooden structures, many of them in the Italian style, which constrasted with the clear winter-sky. Though looking out on the splendid sea, with its ever mellow breath, the eye may forget the northern climate, yet, as I felt very chilly, I could not help remarking, that the lightly built-houses, surrounded by uncovered galleries and open treeless grounds,* seemed little adapted to a latitude, where I was told the summer is as hot as I experienced the winter to be cold. Yet the Americans, who accompanied us, seemed not to find this objectionable, obviously as little caring for

* Americans, in general, do not like trees round their houses.

the trying influences of cold and heat as for food and for rest; they have no standard of cold suitable to our more sensitive nerves.

The scenery of Staten Island, though deprived of foliage, and the warm hue of summer, appeared very pretty. Undulating hills, crowned by nice abodes, and well wooded slopes, make it most attractive, yet it cannot claim the rare mixture of grandeur and loveliness so striking in the Isle of Wight; it is tamer and less varied; the lines of the heights are gentle but monotonous; it offers no picturesque landscapes, though a most delightful site. Many of the citizens of New York have built here abodes in the most varied and grotesque taste. Here an Italian villa, with an oriental veranda; there a Byzantine façade, with a pointed Gothic steeple; yonder on the hill a wooden house, with heavy ornaments, *à la renaissance;* and below in the valley a Swiss cottage, with two lions or tigers, or something between both, a fierce quadruped of the artist's own creation, guarding the doorposts. As there is yet ground enough for the erection of many a building, the island may grow a motley sample of architectural specimens, and may thus at first sight impress the traveller with what architecture is in the States,—a chaotic conglomeration of all styles and all tastes, thrown together as if by chance. But we must confess this style has been introduced from England, and Regent Street and Trafalgar Square remain unsurpassed in that respect all over the world.

Our party moved on slowly over the slopes, followed by numbers of schoolboys and girls. They threw nosegays and wreaths into our carriage, and loudly exulted, when some of them succeeded in getting up the steps and in peeping into our faces.

Interesting as were the gay scenes around, yet we thought the trip rather long, especially considering that Kossuth had to prepare his address to the people of New York for the ensuing day, and that, since our arrival, he had not been left to himself one single moment. He likewise requested the gentlemen to shorten the tour, yet nothing could damp their enthusiastic zeal, to exhibit to us every locality of the Island, and especially to exhibit the "great Hungarian" to everybody: and so we had to drive along the whole circuit.

When, at last, we sat at the dinner-table, feeling quite at home in the amiable family-circle of our kind host, we thought the task of the day accomplished. But the meal was hardly over, when in poured ladies and gentlemen, and Mr. A. A., and Mrs. B. B., and her daughters, and the daughter's cousin, and the cousin's sister, and Mr. D. D., and young Mr. D. D., were introduced, till we had fairly gone through the whole alphabet.

At last the busy hum of the first day of hospitable reception was over, and we went to rest; tired, but grateful for the sympathy which greeted us as friends, and kindly strove to make us forget that we were homeless exiles.

II. RECEPTION IN NEW YORK.
SATURDAY, Dec. 6th.

Dec. 6th.—The sun shone this morning as splen-
didly as yesterday, but to-day I was so fortunate as
not to see its rising, for our sleep was not disturbed by
cannonades in our honour. When I approached the
window I was fascinated with the view on the wonderful bay, peopled by the steam-boats which carry commerce and life to and from its islands and cities. But
soon voices were heard below, and I was summoned to
breakfast. I found the parlour occupied by militia
and navy officers, the former belonging to the Rich-
mond county-guards, the same corps that received
and attended La Fayette at his visit in the United
States, the latter were of the Mississippi steam-frigate,
which carried Kossuth and his family from Ghemlik
to Gibraltar, the deputation of the Reception Committee from New York, and numbers of other visitors
were likewise present, and introductions and speeches
succeeded one another.

Most of the inhabitants of Staten Island and many
other gentlemen, amongst whom we were delighted
to greet Mr. Stiles, late United States minister at
Vienna, accompanied us to the boat which was
ready to convey us to New York. The presence of
Mr. Stiles, and our conversation with him on bygone
times, when Hungary sought his mediation before
the entry of Windischgrätz in Pesth, strongly brought
before my mind our struggles and sufferings, and

when I heard now the hurraing shouts of joy, bursting from the masses, and re-echoing by roars of cannon and peals of music, I could not help feeling very sad, and when I looked at Kossuth and his wife, close to whom I chanced to stand, I saw that their impression was similar to my own.

We were pushed hard before we could get through the crowd on board the Vanderbilt, a most elegant steamer, ornamented by the star-spangled banner, unfolding above the Hungarian tricolour, and the Turkish crescent. But we had little leisure to admire the sumptuous decorations, gildings, mirrors, and tapestries of the boat which carried us; we were too much interested in the panorama along the shores as we steamed about the bay, and in succession got the views of Jersey city, Brooklyn, Williamsburgh, and New York, which proudly adorn the estuary of the Hudson, and are connected by the ever-running ferry-boats into one colossal city. As we moved on and passed the navy yard, with its stately men-of-war, we recognised amongst them the Mississippi. All the masts and all the yards were peopled with seamen and mariners, who shouted and hurraed uninterruptedly, whilst our steamer came up, and the ferry-boats blew their whistles, and the flags of America and Hungary greeted us on every masthead and from many a sail. The animated groups of vessels incessantly roared with cannonades, which our ship returned, mingling this thundering bass to the loud music of the band on board. When we turned from

Jersey city towards Castle Garden and the Battery, our eyes were caught by hundreds and hundreds of glittering swords and regimentals, and masses of people seemed to swell all along the shore. A chaotic noise of vociferation received our steamer when it halted at some yards from the Castle Garden. In fact, the waters were shallow, and anxiety to be the first to step ashore, kept so large a mass of passengers to one side, that it became impossible to land for a considerable time. At last many of the party got out in small boats, and about noon we debarked at the Battery on Manhattan Island. The military formed an avenue through which we were to pass to the hall of Castle Garden, where the people assembled to hear Kossuth. But though our gentlemen, and several officers of the navy and the aldermen who accompanied us, did their very best to shield us, it proved all in vain. The military flourished their swords about to protect us; but the crowd pushed them so vigorously, that there was real danger that we should be hurt by that gallant defence. Nothing could resist the pressure from without, even Lieutenant Nelson, endowed not only with a commanding Kentuckian frame, but likewise with the hardy spirit of his country, could not prevent Madame Kossuth from being repeatedly torn from his arm. At last we emerged on a platform, to which we were raised by invisible agencies. Before us stood Kossuth and the Mayor and several other gentlemen of the Committee; under us numberless heads moved to and fro, and above, people seemed intent to break down the rows of galleries which surrounded the hall, for they thronged and pressed forward, and then there seemed below and above and from all sides, a rush towards Kossuth, so spontaneous as if an electric shock pushed every one a-head. The mayor attempted to speak, but his accents were drowned in thundering hurras, the aldermen gestured, and some of the marshals raised their sticks, adorned with Hungarian rosettes, but all without effect, the rush continued and the cheers swelled to tumultuous uproar. "What do they want?" inquired I from one of the gentlemen. "They are all so very anxious to hear the great Patriot," was the reply. "Then they do not apply the most direct means of getting what they want; how is any man to make himself heard in such turmoil;" this was my remark in a moment, when the flood of excitement seemed to give way. But I had no leisure to hear or see what ensued, because one of the marshals said to us, "Now, ladies, you had better get out to the carriages; you will not be able to break through afterwards." And as we had no inclination to "break through" again, we at once followed the advice, and by a back door, safely got to the carriage, which we occupied with Mr. Pulszky and Lieutenant Nelson. We had now time to survey all the decorations, and the spectators assembled on the spot from whence the procession was to start.

A long row of carriages extended from the corner

of the Battery, near Bowling Green, to the triumphal
arch erected at the beginning of Broadway. The arch
was decorated with the colours of Hungary, inter-
mixed with the star-spangled banner and the Turkish
crescent, which floated above the arms of New York,
bequeathed to this city by its embryo—New Amster-
dam. The Dutch sails of a windmill, two whiskey
barrels, and the beaver skin—those emblems of the
original Dutch settlement, and of the means by which
the fur trade was carried on, and the extermination
of the Indians was achieved—remain still the arms of
the "Empire City." At our right, the cavalry
galloped to and fro along the alleys of Castle Garden, and the infantry drew up in long lines. The
windows of all the houses before us were filled with
people; the bricks of the roofs and the twigs of the
trees seemed to have all become alive, on every
branch perched scores of children. Great masses
of gentlemen in black coats, others in workmen's
attire, covered the whole extent of Battery Place, and
crowded about the garden, while the police and the
marshals were incessantly shouting "Room for the
carriages, gentlemen! Gentlemen, if you please,
room for the carriages!" Several ladies and gentlemen, and workmen, came up to our carriage,
and almost every one of them addressed to us the
question, "How do you like America, is it not a
great country?" To which we of course answered,
that "what we see is very fine indeed, but that we
landed only yesterday on American soil." But this

conclusive answer seemed not to give satisfaction, because the bystanders repeatedly put the same question. One man came up to us, and said that he likewise was a refugee, a German, driven to America in 1848; that he now kept a shop, and liked it very well, and should be glad to receive us at his shop, and to tell us all about New York; and he was anxious to know what we thought about it, and how we had borne the passage, and so on. We could not get rid of him, till the Alderman requested, with some authority, that he should leave us alone, and I thought,—certainly, not only the Americans *born* are inquisitive! either the emigrants at once become Americans, or there is in the very air across the ocean some influence that stimulates curiosity.

An Alderman, who in the mean time was introduced to us, now pointed to the military forming into line, and joining the procession before us. I was struck by the soldier-like appearance of the militia; they certainly looked as if the regimentals were their daily garb; nothing stiff in their bearing, nothing awkward in their movements, they appeared fully disciplined. And when I glanced around on the vigorous, sturdy countenances of the young men, I noticed that every one of them looked quite as soldier-like as the militia; and, therefore, when the Alderman asked me whether I found the aspect of the masses different from that of the English, I replied, " Yes, this people look as if they were more generally pervaded by a military spirit." " And yet we are as fond

of peace as the English," he said. "Well," answered
I, "of that I cannot judge, but it has nothing to do
with a military spirit; this is not necessarily aggres-
sive, but is self-confident; and, therefore, people pervaded by it, look conscious that they can themselves
defend their own rights, and need no large and
expensive standing army." "England, likewise, has
but a small standing army," remarked the Alderman.
"Yes," said I; "but she trusts, it appears to me,
more to the acknowledged power of her fleet to prevent any attack, than to the military spirit of her
people, who look like citizens conscious of their commanding wealth and civilisation, but quite convinced
that they are not likely to be ever called upon to
defend their hearths." "Have you been long in
England? you speak English with great ease," again
asked the Alderman. "I was in England about
two years." "And you?" he continued, turning to
Mr. Pulszky; who replied, that he had resided there
yet longer, and consequently was familiar with the
language. "And do you also speak our language?"
continued the inquisitive Alderman, addressing Lieut.
Nelson; "I calculate I do," was the answer. "Certainly you appear to talk with perfect facility; is it
long since you have learnt it? and where have you
been taught so well?" "In my father's house, about
twenty-six years ago," retorted the officer. The
Alderman looked quite perplexed at the young man,
and exclaimed, "How so! is English taught to in-
fants in Hungary?" "This I don't know," replied

Lieut. Nelson, "but I learnt it in Kentucky;" and, pointing to his coat, said, "Don't you know your own navy?"

We laughed that our Kentuckian friend had, *by his language*, been mistaken for a Hungarian, and found that the Alderman had certainly much flattered us for our knowledge of foreign tongues.

"Where is he? which is the Governor?" was now shouted from all sides, and all eyes turned towards the alley from which Kossuth issued on horseback, accompanied by General Sandford and his staff, after their inspection of the troops. The whole procession preceded us, and therefore I could learn nothing more of it than the description given in the newspapers. But even had they not recorded its pompous length, I should have been fully aware of it by the time it lasted before our carriage began to move, and then it only advanced a few paces, to stop and wait again. Yet, during the slow progress, we had enough to see : flags, with the most varied inscriptions of welcome and sympathy, waved from every roof and every window, and others were suspended across the way; evergreens and red and white roses encircled the 'door-arches, whilst hundreds of stores were adorned with the Hungarian colours, and the portraits of Kossuth, Washington, and Lafayette. The American Eagle spread its wings over the numerous decorations in which the names of Washington and Kossuth were coupled. The Sultan, backed by the British Lion, was likewise triumphantly represented as the noble champion of liberty; and the Russian Bear, and the rescuing Mississippi, and the hospitable Humboldt, every one held a place in this public acknowledgment of universal interest in the fate of the great Patriot.

The finest view of the city we got that day was, when we reached the American Museum. The open space of the Park then relieved the eye from the rows of high buildings through which we had passed. Before us extended the straight line of Broadway, second in length only to Oxford Street, but surpassing it in regularity of buildings, and especially in the magnificence of the hotels. The large square, called the Park, which extends before the City Hall, appeared as the centre of the crowd, which overflowed all the places and streets of New York.

On the steps of the City Hall was a tricolour canopy, to which Kossuth was led. Hardly had he stepped from the carriage, when such thronging and such tumultuous uproar began, that I felt quite bewildered, and expected every moment to see our carriage and all those which preceded us swept away by the multitude. I hardly know what ensued, for the confusion and noise grew every moment, and the crowd obstructed our view in all directions. After a stormy hour we at last began to move again, and slowly passed along the line formed by the brilliant militia, offering a most striking variety of nationalities and regimentals. The American rifles, who never miss their aim, and never retreat before fire; English hussars on fine horses, and again hussars with hel-

mets and epaulets; Irish volunteers, with their
animated countenances and dark hair, finely relieved
by their green coats; the Washington guards, in the
old style, with blue and buff coats, high boots, and
powdered wigs and tails, recalling vividly bygone
times, that we well might fancy they were relics of
the revolutionary war; the German grenadiers, and
stern black rifles—formed altogether a most impres-
sive and varied picture.

It grew almost dark before we had achieved the
whole circuit up Broadway and down Bowery. We
reached the Irving-House by a back-door, for the
front entrance was obstructed by the crowd. Yet
the stairs and passages of this large hotel were likewise beset by gazers; it seemed as if gazing had
become the business of the occasion, for everybody
was everywhere on the look-out, even where I could
not detect anything worth glancing at, and therefore
I was much pleased to retire to the dining-room,
where the mayor, as president of our meal, expected
us.

I was greatly amused, that only black waiters
attended us at table. They all looked very smart
and clean, in white jackets and aprons, and I noticed
with great interest the shining black faces, and the
prominent rolling eyes, beaming with a most jolly
expression of self-satisfaction, especially with one of
them, whose hair was *frisé* straight up and trimmed
with as much care as the beard of King Shalmanassar,
in the British Museum. The lighter coloured Mulatto,

apparently one of the head-waiters, had an air of condescending superiority, fully acknowledged by his black subordinates, who busied themselves with great precision around the table.

In the drawing-room we found a whole bazaar of beautiful nosegays and wreaths. The profusion of flowers in the room, and the love of the ladies for flowers, struck me ever since our arrival on the American shores. In every parlour we entered, bouquets ornamented the vases on the tables, and we hardly met a lady, who did not offer us flowers; they seem here necessary articles for every elegant house, and an indispensable appendage of a hospitable welcome.

In spite of the darkness, the movement and the noise in the street below continued and increased, when suddenly one mass of light illuminated Broadway to a considerable distance. It was a torchlight procession of the Germans and the Turner Society,* distinguished from the surrounding crowd by their white attire, which gives them the appearance of a company of millers, who have been just handling their flour. These associations, which, during the great movement against Napoleon in 1815, did so much to keep up the spirit and the energies of the German fatherland, are now prohibited everywhere in their native country, and it is only across the ocean that they can freely associate, and freely sing

* A Society for gymnastic exercise; the name is derived from tournament.

the patriotic tunes which once called their countrymen
to the defence of their hearths, and which now unite
them again on distant shores. Their band struck up
a march under our windows, but its sounds were lost
in the deafening whirl of a confusion of shouts, and
a storm of impatienee seemed to be roused, as
Kossuth, who was engaged with a deputation from
Philadelphia, did not come to the balcony. One of
the American gentlemen spoke to the masses, trying
to quiet them, but no silence could be obtained. Mr.
Pulszky then appeared, who with his Hungarian hat,
luckily was taken for Kossuth; and as the words he
addressed to the crowd could not be heard in the loud
chorus of cheers and hurras, he made no farther effort
to explain who was who, he bowed low, and waved his
hat, and the crowd was satisfied; but the noise and
talk, and the roars and laughter, and the buzz of the
multitude, continued long after we had retired.

III. NEW YORK SOCIETY, ARCHITECTURE, AND MEETINGS.

(*From Mrs. Pulszky's Diary.*)

Dec. 9th.—When on Sunday we drove to St. Bartholomew's Church, the fine streets of New York looked
quiet and sober in comparison with what they had
appeared on the previous day. The houses, before so
gaudily and gaily apparelled, stood in silent uniformity,
their long lines now unbroken by decorations. Compared with London, but few squares and terraces refresh
the eye, and no magnificent park breathes health

around. It is very remarkable, that whilst the American cities generally command plenty of room, and therefore their houses could easily have been so disposed as to leave ample space for pleasure-grounds, they seem to be avoided as superfluous. And yet the trees along the avenues, and the creepers clustering up the walls of the most elegant houses, show that the Anglo-Saxon race is not less partial to green spots and fresh blossoms across the ocean, than their ancestors were in once merry old England.

The sermon in the Episcopalian Church, which we attended, was dogmatical, and therefore appealing exclusively to the reasoning faculties, and neither calming the mind nor bedewing the feeling. Such sermons are very different from those we were accustomed to hear in Hungary, where they generally preach on moral topics addressed to the heart and imagination, thus leading to contemplation, instead of arousing ideas of controversy. After service was over, I had leisure to see the congregation, which was so numerous that people could get out but slowly. No characteristical costumes mark here the different grades of society, which, in Eastern Europe, impress the foreigner at once with the varied occupations and habits of an old country. There is the peasant girl with the gaudy ribbons interlaced in her long tresses, her bright corset and her richly-folded petticoat; there the Hungarian peasant with his white linen shirt, and his stately sheepskin; the Slovak in the closely fitting jacket and the bright yellow buttons;

the farmer with the high boots and the Hungarian
coat; the old women with the black lace cap in the
ancient national style, and none but the young ladies
apparelled in French bonnets and modern dresses.
But here all have submitted to the rule of Paris
fashion, despotically swaying over Western Europe
and across the Atlantic; they all wear the uniforms
prescribed by English tailors and French milliners.
One gentleman passes after the other, every one of
them clad so exactly alike, that they seem cast in one
and the same mould, and the ladies wear the same
bonnets, the same silk dresses and furs, only varied
in colour, but equal in cut, equal in adornment.
There is no individual turn of mind impressed on the
outward appearance, and therefore such an assembly
bears a manufactured, thoroughly unartistical stamp,
in singular contrast to the poetical beauty of the
ladies. In Europe, I always had understood, that
American women were very pretty up to twenty, but
that their bloom was soon gone. Here, on the contrary, I beheld a whole congregation of attractive
countenances, and though certainly many of them
had passed the prime of youth, the charm of beauty
had by no means departed from their faces.

We proceeded to the house of Mayor Kingsland,
and enjoyed a quiet Sabbath in his amiable family
circle. It was numerous, as families generally are
in America, where people marry young, and where
society is in the happy state that many children are
considered great blessings, and not great cares, as is

generally the case on the continent of Europe. And this, as I often had opportunity to remark in America, is not owing only to the greater facility of getting employment for them, but more especially to the rational view that young men have to push their own way, and that after they have got the benefit of a good education, they are not to depend on their parents for support. Therefore, it is not only the son of the poor and of the little educated families who must look forward *to make himself a man,* but in all classes we meet *self-made men,* who, in consequence, are independent not only in position and fortunes, but likewise by their practical experience, and who, for this very reason, become fit to be self-governed citizens.

Mr. Kingsland is likewise such a self-made man. When yet a boy of fourteen he engaged in business, and, beginning with a small capital, he now, in the prime of manhood, commands ample possessions; and yet each of his sons, so he told me, must choose some profession, for nothing is more despicable and unfortunate, he said, than men without occupation—a life of mere pleasure kills enjoyment.

Mrs. Kingsland, a mother of nine children, is one of those who by youthful appearance denies the prejudice that the bloom of American ladies is but short; and I have since found so frequently mothers of large families whom I mistook for the sisters of their daughters, that I may affirm, that their household cares do not wear them out.

And yet I have heard with them so frequent complaints of the difficulty in managing servants, that the task of a housewife might seem Herculean indeed. I know one instance, where the lady with whom we dined excused herself for the imperfections of the meal she offered us, by the circumstance that her cook had left her just as the dinner was going to be prepared. "Without any previous notice?" inquired I, astonished. "Oh, she did it on purpose to annoy me," was the answer, "because I had repeatedly found fault with her management. It is a sad thing with us, seriously interfering with our domestic comfort, that we cannot get an attendant to remain with us any length of time; they think nothing of changing places, ever so often."

"But do not the masters think it very unsafe," I remarked, "to take people who have not the recommendation of steady characters? If those who leave service for any petty reason could not find employment again without considerable difficulty, they would take good care not to run away."

"No doubt that this would be a check," answered the lady, "but then there is the difficulty of getting servants—the demand is larger than the supply."

"Is this the case likewise here in New York?" asked I, "where emigrants abound, and would be glad to earn something before they proceed farther into the country?"

"The emigrants who come here willing to serve," continued the lady, "are either ragged Irish, filthy

and negligent, and therefore little desirable as servants, or Germans, generally small farmers or poor
mechanics, whose daughters at home had been accustomed only to the meanest housework, and are but
little adapted to attend to a larger and more refined
establishment; and the worst, they are impertinent,
because they know that we cannot do without them."

"Excuse me," said I, interrupting my amiable
friend, "this is the point—*that they know you cannot
do without them*. If cooking, sewing, washing, &c.,
were to form elements of the practical education of
an American lady, she would seldom be called upon
to leave her piano for the kitchen fire, and she would
have good servants. The uneducated are like children, who instinctively feel whom they have to deal
with, and who obey only those who are consistent
and just in their orders, and it is obviously impossible to be either consistent or just in the direction of
a work we do not understand."

The lady acknowledged the truth of this assertion,
but objected that her daughters, for example, were
initiated in the domestic arts, of which our meal was
an evidence, which they had dressed themselves; but
that the servants were so accustomed, by the general
habit, not to be told of anything, that they would not
submit to the slightest reproof, and that, in consequence, she often had to change her cooks from six
to ten times in a year.

Of course it is difficult for individuals to counteract
an evil which is rooted, as it seems to me, *partly* in

the accidental circumstances of the country, but much more still in certain habitual prejudices and customs. That employment is more accessible, and that thrifty people can more easily keep up their hearth in the United States than in Europe, are facts which necessarily diminish the competition of servants; but the prejudice which I have found very much spread in America, that the female sex is honoured by being expected *not to work,* and the custom to attach a selfish meaning to " independence," viz., *"every one for himself,"* certainly acts much more to demoralize the servants and to discomfort the masters than any other influence.

It is a common boast with American gentlemen, that their ladies rule, and are more respected than anywhere else in the world. I heard this often repeated in the society of New York, and I inquired of a gentleman, who was repeating this pet phrase, in what way they ruled? " Why, they have all they like," was the reply: " they dress and go shopping, and have not to care about anything; we even live in hotels, to save them the trouble of housekeeping."

" I see," observed I, " you are almost as courteous as the Turks, who allow their wives every amusement in their harems, and about the shops, whilst they attend to graver matters. The elegantly-gilded and painted parlours of your hotels, where the ladies meet to rock away time in the easy rocking-chairs, are admirable harems; but what has all this to do with *the rule* of your ladies? Even granted that you

accepted their wishes as commands, still you are no
Pashas whose whims claim obedience from the community; you, yourselves, rule only by the active part
you take in public affairs, and do you mean to say
you consult your ladies about these matters?"

"Well, not exactly," answered the gentleman;
"but, (said he) a lady can travel alone all over the
States without danger of an insult, or unbecoming
behaviour; our daughters go often out, and are in
society without their mothers,—every man is their
natural protector."

"Quite as in Turkey," replied I; "no man, not
even the husband, would ever dare to follow his veiled
lady in the streets, and if he sees a slipper before the
door of her room, the sign that another lady visits
her, not even the Pasha presumes to intrude.   And
as to the travels of the unprotected ladies, they are
perhaps less frequent in Europe than in America, but
the manners and customs of our age protect them as
efficiently in the old as in the new world.   All the
difference perhaps is, that the morality in the United
States, is more sterling than in France and Italy, or
in the capitals of Austria and Russia, and therefore
flirtations with married ladies are unheard of."

"But in Europe," he said, "women even work in
the fields, and they must assist the husbands to earn
subsistence for their families; with us, even in the
factories, the girls work until they marry, but once
married, the maintenance of the family is the care of
the husband, and an American farmer would feel

degraded, if his wife or daughter should hoe the corn or break the flax."

Of course, I readily acknowledged, that owing to the greater facilities of earning a livlihood, the women of the lower classes were much better off than in Europe, but I did not understand in what way the respect for the fair sex is connected with this fact. The gentleman turned to other topics; I sought information on the other side, and understood from some very intellectual ladies, that their lords, *in general*, little consult the opinions of their female rulers, even as concerns their own private affairs. I learnt, that it occurs but too often, that a lady who believes herself to be in affluent circumstances, is suddenly informed by her husband that they must give up housekeeping, because they cannot afford it. It appears as if the gentlemen would atone for their all-absorbing *passion for business*, by the privilege they give to the ladies of idling their time away. And as *business* is a passion with the Americans,—as business is with them not the means, but the very life of existence, they are most anxious to keep this department *exclusively* to themselves; and, well aware that there is no more infallible way to secure non-interference, than by giving the general impression that they never act for themselves, *the lady's rule* has become a current phrase, but by no means a fact in the United States.

Dec. 11*th*.—Yesterday we went shopping with

some ladies, and visited the most elegant resorts of
shawls, silks, lace, millinery, and jewellery. I tried
to get some American material for dresses; but their
national prints are so gaudy in colour, and comparatively so expensive, that I do not wonder that French
and English silks form the habitual apparel of American
ladies. They seem to be very extravagant in this respect, for we hardly met one lady in Broadway without
light-coloured rich silks, such as in Paris we are only
wont to see at evening parties; and they wear plumed
bonnets, with which they would look much better in
elegant coaches along the alleys of a park, than
among the pedestrians of the dusty pavement at New
York. And there they walk with very thin shoes,
unmindful of the cold from which they shield their
necks by ample furs, but their delicate feet remain
unprotected by the double soles with which English
ladies are wont to steer bravely through the wet and
mud. Such expeditions American ladies greatly
shun, and it is only on very clear days that they venture even so far as Broadway, and seldom without a
carriage to cover their retreat.

Shopping and calls seem here, as well as in London,
considerable items in the expenditure of time with
the ladies. Their hours are altogether earlier than
in England; their occupations, exercise in the open
air excepted, much the same as in the mother country. They attend public beneficent institutions, read
whatever publishers or newspapers recommend to
their attention, write as many letters as they can

think of, play some waltzes, and, even occasionally, the Yankee Doodle, or the Star-spangled Banner; copy modern prints or some landscape with very blue lakes, very green trees, and remarkably violet mountains; or instead of the brush, they use the needle, and embroider similarly gaudy objects on a screen or cushion. The household affairs interfere but little with the visits, lectures, concerts and theatres, and a good deal of sociable gaiety is mixed up with this life of fashion amongst the ladies in New York. In the summer months they habitually desert town for their country seats on the Hudson, or they make a trip to Europe, but more often to Saratoga or some other watering place; excursions to Mobile and New Orleans are not unfrequent with the ladies of New York, whose nerves seem to shrink from cold, at least judging by their rooms, where they keep up a temperature perfectly insupportable to us. In that respect their passages and fine mahogany stairs are much more inhabitable than their apartments, because there the stoves diffuse equal warmth, whilst here the chimneys and Manchester carpets add an oppressive surplus of heat. And yet their houses are much less cage-like than in London; the drawing-rooms, library, and dining-room, though spacious, are often on the same floor, whilst the bed-rooms and nurseries alone occupy the upper stories. And the nurseries form by no means the exclusive realm of the children: they roam about the house, upstairs and down, circulating freely like little birds not confined to cages, but

fluttering about the whole precinct of an ample hot-
house. And thus the little ones are not abandoned
to the nurses, but the mother has them constantly
under her eye, though I cannot say under her control, for they have their own way, they run in and
out, and play tumbling and dragging about books and
cushions and chairs, and climbing up and down just
as they please. In consequence they never are
embarassed, and meet every one who chances to come
with the most perfect ease. Unconstrained, and not
pre-occupied by any conventional rule, they grow
strikingly sharp, and answer to every enquiry with a
self-dependence and self-observation which never can
be obtained by a training to accepted notions and
habitual manners. But on the other side, such children, unaccustomed to check and to control their
impulses, easily become spoiled to all discipline, and
this explains in a great measure the habit prevalent
in America, of placing even the girls at school, thus
depriving the mother of her most precious privilege
to educate her own daughter. Of course, when the
little girl, simply abandoned to her inclinations, is
never made conscious that she has to adapt herself to
anything but her own disposition, the mother rarely,
if ever, will have the energy and firmness to check
the growing torrent of passions, stronger in proportion
as the child gets older. And more than that, a
mother who herself, in her early youth, has not been
impressed with the necessity of obedience, which is
the beginning and the great end of all education, can

never develop the faculties of her daughter, and adapt them to the various circumstances of life.

But why should the schoolmistress understand this better, is the question which naturally suggests itself. The schoolmistress may often be as little adapted to the art of education as the mother herself; and, as we see from their prospectuses, they likewise hardly profess to give *education,* but simply offer large doses of all kinds of *instruction.* But in a place where many are to be taught, to be fed, and to be accommodated under one roof, discipline does not only spring from the theoretical rules of the house, but is the practical result of the exigencies of a variety of children compelled to live together from morning to night. The rougher their tempers are the more they will clash, but the more, likewise, they will chastise and correct each other; and thus the school itself, independent of the teacher, may remedy, to a certain extent, the neglect of discipline in early age.*

Dec. 14th.—To-day a quiet Sunday again; most welcome amidst busy New York, where during the week every one seems to rush and to run, and is very impatient when his passage is stopped by the coaches

* Later I had also the good fortune to meet with some ladies, engaged as directors of schools, who are admirably adapted, by their talents and devotion, to this sacred calling. Their own personal influence on their establishment is such as to satisfy a mother's heart who places her darling there. But these ladies are exceptions; they give to their pupils education, whilst generally they get but instruction.

and omnibuses, and the cars running on the horse-
railways through the town. And from dawn till
dusk, and long after, still the carriages roll, how long
I do not know, for I always fall asleep before their
busy commerce has ceased. But to-day the thorough-
fares are turned into walks, where people saunter
about at leisure, following the tinkle of the bells, and
the strains of the organs, calling them into churches
of the most different denominations: Episcopalians,
Presbyterians, Baptists, Lutherans, Moravians, Con-
gregationalists, Methodists, Roman Catholics, Uni-
versalists, Jews, Friends, Unitarians, Swedenborgians;
and the emigrants too of all nations, with holiday-
coats worn out, relics of their distant homes, enjoy
the bright morning rays of the sun. To-day they do
not look out for work, with anxious care, for to-day
is the day of rest,—and rest to the body grants hope
to the mind.

We were driving beyond the outskirts of New York
to the Harlem-valley, and along our path we noticed
detached cottages all of wood. Across the river,
more solid abodes rise here and there, country-seats,
I understand, but not to be compared in size or style
to our feudal stone mansions in Europe. Wherever
a couple of houses stand within the compass of half a
mile, a steeple rises, and sometimes we see even two
churches where there are no more than two houses
close by; but the inhabitants belong to different
denominations, and therefore attend different places
of worship.

The landscape expands, and presents a picture of rural solitude, as we approach the aqueduct of the Croton water, the high bridge, which is boldly thrown across the Harlem-valley, here a quarter of a mile wide—and the river of the same name—620 feet in breadth. This structure of solid granite singularly contrasts with the tame scenery around, and impresses one with a feeling of respectful awe for the energetic men who raised such a monument, solid and grand like the rocks of the mountains; and yet it forms only one link to the great chain of dams, canals, and reservoirs, which supply the town with water, so amply requiring it, not only for its most immediate use, but likewise not less to extinguish the conflagrations, which are so habitual that, except the firemen, no one seems to care for them, least of all the owners of the burning houses, who have always taken good care not to insure them under their value.

"Is it not a Roman work?" asked one of our American companions. "Roman, indeed," said an Englishman present, with a sneer; "your engineers seem to have forgotten the hydrostatic law, which the Romans never knew, that water in connected tubes rises everywhere to the same level. In England we carry the water with less architectural beauty, but at smaller cost, over hill and dale, simply upon this principle."

Dec. 16*th.*—The architecture of New York is the common street architecture of London; in fact, it is no

style whatever. Though we do not meet with those dark
rows of brick buildings without any decoration, built
with no other purpose than that of investing money,
and of getting a good rent, without any feeling for
beauty, or even for ornaments; yet the same defi-
ciency of original forms, and of harmonising proportions, which makes the streets of London so
monotonous, is found likewise here in America. The
houses are generally built on one and the same plan ;
they have no individuality. It seems the creative
power has ceased entirely with the architects of our
age; they either do not care anything about the
external beauty of the houses, or, in the best case,
they copy with servile accuracy some ancient building, often without reference to the position of the
original. More often they patch up different parts
of classical buildings of all styles in an eclectic way,
which unavoidably destroys the effect, as is the case
with the City Hall. On the whole the houses are
more substantial than in London. The brick-build-
ings of the fifth avenue (the West-end of New York)
are superior to those in Belgravia, and many granite
and marble façades bear evidence, that the architect
was not controlled by parsimony in the proprietor,
and that it is probably not the fault of the latter if
the wooden staircases are so narrow that two persons
cannot pass at once, whilst on the continent of
Europe the staircase becomes the ornament of the
palace. The house most elegantly fitted up is un-
questionably that of Mr. Haight, with an Italian

winter garden, playing fountains, large saloons in the Parisian fashion, a drawing-room in the style of the Taj Mahal at Agra, a splendid library, &c. &c. You perceive at once that the owner of the house has travelled all over Europe, and likes to be surrounded with the recollections of everything he has seen abroad. The churches have nothing peculiar; modern church architecture is yet poorer than the street architecture, and not only the artist, who, in those times which we call the dark ages, built the unparalleled cathedrals, which for the beauty of proportions, and richness of decorations, remain the unequalled wonders of art; but even Palladio and his immediate scholars are unrivalled in our days.

But in the south part of New York we have beautiful temples, some of white marble, others of dark granite, evidently copies of the monuments of Athens. And who is the god whom they adore in those graceful structures? what shrine is it that occupies the place of Athenè Parthenos, and of the Olympian Jupiter? It is god Mammon, to whom they have raised those temples; it is the almighty Dollar which is worshipped in those noble halls. This splendid amphistyle temple, with the forest of Doric columns, it is the *Exchange*—this other, the *Custom House*—and those graceful prostyle buildings, they are *Banks*.

We had a most pleasant dinner party, where we met Washington Irving, whose name, ever since I have been acquainted with English literature, was connected in my mind with such genuine freshness of conception, that I fancied the author of the 'Sketch Book,' and of the radiant pictures of the Alhambra, must remain always young. I was, therefore, rather childishly surprised to see a gentleman, on whose lofty brow years have impressed their traces, and to hear that he was the man whom my imagination had endowed with the unwithering vigour of youth, like Goëthe, whose Jupiter frame was not bent by age. But, listening to his conversation, full of hope and warmth, I found that my early impression had not been wrong. Washington Irving can as little grow old as his works—their covers may be worn out, but never their contents.

Dec. 19*th.*—It was a dark and chilly evening, when Mr. Levitt, the great banker of Brooklyn, whose wealth is connected with the prosperity of the city, —as the owner of large tracts of land in Long Island, bought before the city had extended on them,—came to take us there to a meeting, which was to congregate at the Plymouth Church. Whilst we drove to the Fulton Ferry, Mr. Levitt gave us an account of what Brooklyn had been a generation ago, when he settled there. Then it was a village, now it is a rising city, perhaps shortly a rival of New York, to which it is connected by ferry-boats, so well managed that they carry on the busy intercourse of the city without delay or inconvenience; it is even not necessary to get out of the carriage for steering across the floating bridge.

We found the church crowded, yet there was no pressure or noise; all appeared intent on the words of sympathy for the sacred cause of Hungary, uttered by the Rev. Doctor Bethune and Henry Ward Beecher, the brother of the author of 'Uncle Tom's Cabin.' I was especially struck by the expression of energy in the address of Mr. Beecher, as well as in his countenance, which bears the stamp of the superiority acknowledged to distinguish the members of his family. I have repeatedly heard in New York, that the Beechers have a great influence on the intellectual movement of their country, and though sometimes they are reproached with eccentricity and ultra views, no one disputes their possession of a lofty turn of mind, brilliant talents, and the earnestness of purpose, which never fails to succeed.

After the meeting, we repaired to Mr. Levitt's house, where we were told that we should meet but a very few of his most intimate friends and relatives. These must be numerous, for the large mansion overflowed with people, so as to allow as little room for conversation amidst the bewildering buzz of the assembly, as freedom to movement in the midst of the pressure from all sides. It was as bad as in London, where the attraction of a party is thought to be in inverse proportion to its comfort. In London, a gentleman, who, with his lady hanging on his arm, works hard for three or four hours to thread his unnoticed way through all the apartments, till at last they are swept back to their carriage by the flood of departing guests, has at least his recompense and full share of pleasure on the following day, by reading his name in the 'Morning Post,' amongst the host of titled guests and distinguished foreigners at the delightful party at Lady * * * 's; but here in America it is different, there is no 'Morning Post' to publish the names, and therefore everybody must be introduced to everybody, and everybody must get in, and nobody must be allowed to get out before being presented to the distinguished guest of the evening, whom the party has been invited to meet. So the master of the house gives you his arm, and leads you all round and all through the apartments, and introduces you to innumerable Mr.'s and Mrs.'s and Misses, and even the Masters shake hands with you, until you have forgotten all the new friends who are happy to have made your acquaintance.

This is the general way in which parties are enjoyed, though exceptions are, of course, numerous; and we spent most pleasant evenings in elegant circles, large enough not to centralize conversation, and yet not so thronged as to interfere with the ease, without which no intercourse can be pleasant. I gladly remember the hours spent at several families in New York, especially at Mrs. Bancroft's. Here again I admired the attractive countenances of the majority of the ladies, as fresh and delicate as the blossoms which they wear, and which match their style of beauty uncommonly well. Their evening dress is more French than English, and therefore not so full stocked as to burden their graceful figures, which is the case out of doors, when furs and plumed bonnets, and immense muffs and veils, which they often do not raise even during a call, muffle them up as if they wished to be disguised.

When in the night we returned from Brooklyn, we found the large parlours on the second flight of the Irving House festively illuminated and decorated. The celebration of a marriage was here going on, with fiddling and dancing. The parents of the bride boarded in the house, and I had repeatedly chanced to meet the mother in the passage; she had most cordially invited us, to join their gay assembly, and I now went into the ball-room, to witness what appeared to my European views very odd—nuptials at an hotel! If anything seems, by its nature, entitled to privacy, it is the family circle gathering round a young couple about to leave the paternal roof for their own hearth; and however happy the union, and however bright the prospects of the newly-married pair, they are taking leave of habitual associations, to enter upon a different life. And every farewell of this kind, if not sad, is connected with feelings intimately solemn, shunning the glance of a stranger, and the curiosity of the intruder.

It is true, that in the East likewise, at the occasion of a marriage, the house is thrown open to every one

who wishes to unite in the joy of the festive event,
which thus gets in some respect the character of
publicity; but in the Eastern notion the man who
tastes of your salt and eats of your bread, is no longer
a stranger, hospitality consecrates him at once to a
friend, and for that very reason, though hundreds
may partake of the feast, it never can have anything
common with an entertainment in a public place,
where nobody can be excluded. For though a whole
suite of apartments had been previously secured for
the celebration of the marriage at the hotel, yet the
doors of the parlours remained open, and were beset
by curious gazers.

"Does she not look very pretty?" was the general
remark, pointing to the bride, and then her appearance and the articles of her dress were admired and
commented upon, just as if she were a heroine on
the stage, appearing for public amusement and
criticism.

Really those American hotels, with their communities of boarders, who live there for months and
perhaps for years; meet daily in the parlour and at
the dinner-table, who therefore are not altogether
strangers to one another, though not connected by
any interest or sympathy, most strangely strike every
European. A Frenchman might fancy himself in a
Phalanstére of Mr. Fourier, but I must say I never
could accustom myself to this want of privacy, and
could not understand how it is possible for people
who could have their own homes to live in a hotel.

And yet there are thousands in the United States who always live in the hotels; they marry there, they educate their children there, and die there, without ever having had a private home.

"Is it true that the Governor has received a deputation of coloured persons?" I was asked by a gentleman. I answered that I had heard of such a delegation having called on him.

"But you do not mean to say that he saw them?" continued Mr. * * *.

I expressed my astonishment at the doubt, as I could not understand how Kossuth, whose door was open to any one interested in the cause he pleaded, should shut out people because they were coloured. But my remark seemed to be quite as strange to the gentleman as his opinion appeared to me. To see coloured persons in a drawing-room, was obviously an offence against a prejudice of the aristocracy of colour, as deeply-rooted as the horror of high-born continental ladies for those whose pedigree cannot prove a range of sixteen noble ancestors. I could not refrain to tell to Mr. * * * as a parallel case, that one of those exclusive ladies in Vienna, who often was in want of money, and found herself obliged occasionally to receive a banker who transacted her business—had her drawing-room fumigated as often as that gentleman left it. She found the aristocratic air of her drawing-room was polluted by the breath of low-born persons, who were mere bankers.

But the American could not find out the parallelism
of the case, and thought it monstrous that the relation
of whites to whites should be compared to the relation
of white men, free and equal, to coloured persons of
an inferior race, slaves themselves, or at least the
sons and descendants of slaves. No social intercourse
on the basis of equality is possible with them, even
in the Free States.

But it is not only the white man who looks down
upon the black. From the dark mulatto to the hardly-
tinged quadroon, every lighter shade claims a grade
of preeminence, acknowledged by the full black and
the white. A mulatto girl sewed for me in the
hotel, and I soon remarked that one of the black
waiters attended on her with uncommon courtesy, and
brought her for her dinner every dainty the kitchen
and the cellar afforded, as if ordered by us. I thought
this extravagant, and told it to the housekeeper, who
exclaimed, " The bad girl, to degrade herself so far as
to accept attention from a black fellow !" This,
then, was the great error, not that she had accepted a
bottle of champagne, to which she had no right, but
that she had accepted it *" from the black fellow !"*

Dec. 20th.—Mrs. Kingsland and Dr. and Mrs.
Sayre took us to the Institution for the Blind. In
the countenances of many of the pupils I noticed that
calm and bright expression which proves that there
is the light within which reveals the kindness of the
Creator, though the rays of the sun cannot pierce

through the darkened sense. One young person read
to us a passage of the Scriptures, with such fervency
of faith, that I felt she beheld with the heart what
many do not see who decipher with the eye. Her enthusiasm for the cause of Hungary, and for Kossuth,
was very striking; she warmly pressed Madame
Kossuth's hand, saying, how much she had felt for
her sufferings, and admired her heroism; and her
companions approached and pressed around us, listening with obvious interest. They then assembled
round the piano, and joined in an ode, a welcome to
Kossuth, composed by one of them. I asked what
became of the poorer pupils educated here, after they
leave the institution? and was told that some of them
found employment as teachers in schools for the
blind, others as organists, or as basket-makers. Yet
there is often difficulty for the less advanced and
energetic amongst them to get on, and, in consequence, a work-department had been added to the
·institution, where thirty-three blind persons, male and
female, get constant employment with willow basket-
making, carpet-weaving, and the manufacture of mats,
mattresses, and brooms. The women manufacture
also paper boxes, sew, and do fancy work. The married ones board and lodge at home with their families,
whilst the institution furnishes only a home to those
who cannot do better elsewhere.

Altogether, the whole establishment appears very
practically arranged, managed with perfect regularity, without any superfluous show, which can

nowhere be more ill-placed than in the abode of the blind.

Dec. 21*st.*—The meeting of the ladies in Tripler Hall, enthusiastic for the cause of Hungary and her great Representative, offered to me again a fresh aspect of New York society. The assembly was altogether different from the congregation in Brooklyn. I had the impression that most of those who energetically interrupted Kossuth's appeal to their sympathies with exclamations of approbation, had long been familiar with the merits of our struggle, which they had followed with that fervid interest connected with their remembrance of what their own forefathers had undergone. They seemed to be men working more with the hands than with the head, and, for that very reason, ever ready to stand by a cause they think righteous, without anxious criticism of details and personalities.

But here—so it appeared to me—the majority was composed of the fashionable members of society, whom a foreign cause hardly can rouse, unless embodied in an attractive personality. This impersonation now stood before them, and therefore they were strained to the height of enthusiasm; an enthusiasm, I believe, not quite so transient as might be expected from its nature; for wherever the Anglo-Saxon race prevails, no impression, powerful enough to raise their blood, can ever be easily effaced.

Kossuth, with the instinct of his genius, fully

adapted his discourse to his audience. It was not in powerful features that he pictured the wrongs of his country, he appealed not to the judgment of those who were little familiar with the details of the subject, but he delicately delineated the noble spirit of the fatherland whose children bleed and suffer for its cause. His speech was a beautiful elegy, whose lovely accents swell into tragical pathos, and the key-note was given for the strain of sympathy which thrilled through every heart, and bedewed many an eye.

I was likewise highly interested with the speech of Mr. Bancroft. It was a fine effort of rhetoric, of an almost classical stamp. The conclusion, especially, was of matchless beauty. After having mentioned that it was the colonies of monarchical Greece which first instituted republicanism, and that their example was followed by the mother country, and having expressed his conviction that the time is coming when like causes will have again the same effects ;— "Would you know," he proceeded, " what was the symbol of the near advent of this result? It was when our illustrious friend, sailing under the glorious banner of the Stars and Stripes, the tricolor of America, passed between the isles of Greece, then it was that the Nereides of the Egean Sea clasped their hands for joy ; then the sun looked out with splendour on the Parthenon; then the bees, as they gathered honey on Mount Hymettus, found the flowers possessed of unwonted fragrance ; then the Muses, as they stood disconsolate on Mount Cithæron,

rose up, and pointing to the field of Platæa, exclaimed with a voice to be heard throughout the
world, Aristides, too, was an exile,—and the field of
Platæa keeps the record what a returning exile may
do.　We look to the future then with hope, we are
firm in our belief, that Hungary will emerge from
the lurid clouds which now overhang her; we are
confident that we may yet welcome her in the clear
light of the morning, shining as the star of the East;
shining on the forehead of the morning sky, the
brightest star of the firmament,—the day-star of
republican liberty !"

The Hon. George Bancroft is the late Ambassador
of the United States in England, the celebrated
historian of North America.　He belongs to the
Democratic party, but he is allied, by his amiable
wife, to the principal Whigs in Massachusetts.　His
words give a fair specimen of the view American
statesmen take of the state of things in Europe.

IV. THE PERIODICAL PRESS IN NEW YORK CITY.

The enthusiasm created by Kossuth's arrival was
unmeasured.　Deputations from all parts of the
country, and invitations to all the principal towns of
the Union, arrived daily; it seemed, all classes of
society were anxious to overwhelm him with honours
and kindness, in order to make him forgetful of his
country, and a happy citizen of the United States.

But he openly announced at the first opportunity, that he did not come to seek comforts and a new home, but aid and support in his great enterprise—the liberation of Hungary. The astonishing facility with which he expressed his thoughts in foreign languages, for he had to address deputations not only in English, but also in French, Italian, and German; the dazzling eloquence of his speeches, and the graceful manner in which he delivered them, startled even those professional politicians who did not like his views. The sympathy for the man who had struggled against two mighty empires, who had then been guarded against them by the Sultan at the risk of a war, and at last released by the combined efforts of the two free nations of the West,—was transferred from his person to his cause, the cause of Hungary, the keystone of European liberty. He seemed to be endowed with the gift of tongues: since Peter the Hermit and John Capistran, the world had not looked upon his like. His speech at the Municipal Banquet was universally admired, and the press, the bar, the militia, and the people of Brooklyn, the Democrats of Tammany Hall, the clergy, the students of Columbia College, and the ladies of New York, prepared banquets and meetings, to hear the eloquence of the great foreigner.

The press was full of his praises, and the Conservatives became somewhat alarmed. The 'Courier and Inquirer,' the organ of the silver-grey Whigs and of the Exchange—a paper with a circulation of

about 2,000 copies a day,*—was anxious to involve
Kossuth in a personal polemic.   His attacks, however,
on Hungary and her elected chief were not heeded,
and when the editor endeavoured to prove that
Kossuth had insulted him by denouncing, generally,
the organs of Austrian diplomacy—he was laughed
at.   The first attack had failed.   It was now planned
to cool down the public enthusiasm by associating
Kossuth with unpopular political parties.   The
Abolitionists, of course, paid their respect to the man
who had initiated and carried the emancipation of
the peasantry from the pressure of feudal burdens,
and a deputation of coloured persons came also with
an address greeting the hero of European liberty.

The 'New York Herald' immediately seized the
opportunity for identifying Kossuth with the Abolitionists of Garrison's party, and hinted that he was most
heartily received by Freesoilers and Woolly-heads.
It moreover construed his reception of the coloured
men into a personal insult of a deputation of some
distinguished citizens of Florida.   Kossuth had to
send a circular to the papers saying, that, consistent
with his principle of non-interference with the
domestic affairs of any foreign nation, he naturally
does not enter into any discussion of the American
domestic institutions; and Mr. John Calhoun, the
chairman of the Florida deputation, published a most

---

* It is conducted by General Watson Webb, who was sent by
President Fillmore as Chargé d'Affaires to Vienna, but was recalled
by the Senate, who would not confirm the nomination.

eloquent and elaborate letter in favour of Kossuth's principles. But it was easily to be seen that the 'New York Herald' desired to dam the tide of popular enthusiasm. It is a paper conducted with surprising tact; it has no principles whatever; it takes up and ridicules every question according to its whims, without any scruple; it has but one aim, to increase its circulation, to create excitement, to spread scandals, to make money. The Editor, Mr. Gordon Bennett, has succeeded so far, that the 'Herald' has a circulation of above 30,000 copies. He is an emigrant Scotchman, who hates England, and has no love for America. But he has studied the American character, he admirably flatters the prejudices and delusions of the masses, and has an instinctive aversion against everybody whose motives are not those of money-making. His paper is pervaded by a spirit of negations; nothing is positive with him except his predilection for slavery. His boast is, that he is the enemy of all *isms*, as he calls it; and there are many practical, narrow-minded men in America, who, repeating this slang, think they protest only against mesmerism, socialism, communism, and abolitionism, not aware that the 'Herald' includes in these *isms*, republicanism, protestantism, and patriotism.

The 'New York Tribune' is in every respect a contrast of the 'Herald.' It is the organ of the Seward-fraction of the Whigs, advocating protection of American industry, supporting progress in every shape, giving a fair trial to every new theory, opening its column to every one who thinks himself oppressed, to German philosophers, to French socialist discussions, to the rights of woman, and even to the spiritual manifestations. Mr. Horace Greeley, the editor of this paper, earnestly seeks truth; he is always sincere in his opinions, never evading a question, upright, straightforward, conscientious. The circulation of his journal nearly equals that of the ' Herald,' though Gordon Bennett is better served by his correspondents, and is often a-head with the latest intelligence, and in point of spirited style surpasses the heavier articles of Greeley.

Whilst in polemic the weapons of the ' Herald' are the poison of calumny, and the dagger of treachery,* the ' Tribune' is armed with a club that knocks down his adversaries with rough blows. This paper sways over Western New York, the Northern and North-Western States, and all the back country; you find it everywhere, in the log-houses of the new settlements in Michigan and Wisconsin, in Iowa and Minnesota. The domain of the ' Herald' begins where the ' Tribune' is

* As an instance of the good taste of the ' New York Herald,' we extract the following passage on the expedition to Japan :—"We are glad to hear that the proposed hydrographic survey of Japan is not turned over to the Dutch—glad that the heathen of those islands are not to be abandoned. In these days, nothing but bombshelling and bayonets will reclaim the Pagans of Japan. Let the gallant Commodore hurry up the good work. Brethren, let us pray."—It is to be observed, that the ' New York Herald' *never did oppose the expedition against Japan,* and *that it is really a strong advocate of this measure.*

excluded; it is the paper of the planter of the South, of the fashionable in the great cities, and of the men of society everywhere. All of them say they despise the paper, but they read it and buy it, and Gordon Bennett quotes Vespasian, "Lucri bonus odor ex re qualibat."

The 'Evening Post' is the only democratic paper of New York, edited by the great poet, W. Bryant, and his accomplished son-in-law, Parke Godwin. It is a free-trade paper, and represents the liberal fraction of the democratic party, with free-soil tendencies. The pro-slavery whig paper is the 'Evening Express;' the 'Commercial,' and the 'Journal of Commerce' are written for the banks and offices; but the circulation of all these journals is very limited. The 'Sun' has the largest circulation, it is a cheap journal, written or rather extracted for the masses from all the other papers. The New York 'Daily Times,' also a cheap paper, ranks much higher, and is as widely spread as either of the great journals. It is a liberal Whig publication, less heavy and less theoretical, but not less sincere than the 'Tribune.' The editor, Mr. Will. H. Raymond, an amiable young man, of prepossessing manners, has already been the speaker of the house in the State of New York, and is probably destined to serve his state and his country in many higher positions.

V. TITLES OR NICKNAMES IN THE UNITED STATES.

Nothing is more puzzling for a foreigner in English society than the titles. It is so difficult to know who is who; the son does not bear the name of his father, the younger brother not the name of his older brother, and the wife not always the name of her husband. And then there are lords who are peers, and lords who are not peers; and again lords who are neither peers nor lords, but who are called so by courtesy; there are honourables and right honourables, reverends and right reverends, and nobody knows the real rank and precedency of a Roman Catholic bishop; there are lieutenants who are captains, and captains who are majors, and generals who are colonels, and the sergeants are barristers, and the barons are judges, and everybody is an esquire who wears a good coat, and every esquire who has made his name so prominent that he has at last got a title of nobility, immediately drops the name under which he has become known to the world, as if he was ashamed of his past;—really it is difficult for a foreigner not to make a mistake, or to address everybody in the becoming way.—I thought in America there is no such puzzling distinction in society; but to my great astonishment, I experienced that I had left the titled aristocracy, only to find across the ocean a titled democracy.

Only, instead of the civil titles, military titles prevail in the United States. As to the former, they are but few; the president, the ambassadors, and the governors of the States are addressed "Excellency," during the time of their office; but the governors retain the title of "Governor" for ever. The members of the senate at Washington are titled "Senators" during their term, and are for life styled "Honourables," together with the heads of department, and the members of the House. The same title is given by courtesy to all those who are or were members of the state legislature in either House, and to all the judges, to whose name the designation of "Judge" is also always prefixed in conversation. But all this vanishes if compared with the innumerable military titles. Everybody belongs to the militia, and as the militia chooses the officers by ballot, the number of the militia captains, majors, colonels, and generals, is really legion; and all those captains, majors, colonels, and generals, are always addressed as such, though they are shopkeepers and mechanics, and lawyers and hotel-keepers, and journalists. All the nation is playing at soldiers; but when the war began with Mexico, all those militia officers fought bravely in the battles against a well-disciplined army, led by professional officers, and there is no doubt that a really military spirit pervades the nation.

But the Americans are not only fond of titles, they delight also in nicknames, which are seldom malicious, though a vein of irony is often discernible in them. There is perhaps no prominent man in the

States who would not have a nickname, which in fact
becomes his title of nobility, bestowed on him by the
people. General Jackson was called *Old Hickory*, on
account of his inflexible character; his diplomatic
successor in the White House, Martin Van Buren,
was known as the *Little Magician;* and his son, John
Van Buren, remains until now *the Prince.* General
Harrison was *Old Tip*, an abbreviation of Tippecanoe,
where he had defeated the Indians under their pro-
phet, the brother of Tecumsch. General Zachary
Taylor was designated by the name *Old Zack, Rough-
and-ready;* and Henry Clay, as *the Millboy of the
slashes,* in remembrance of his origin. Webster is
the Great Expounder, the Godlike, or simply *Black
Dan.* Corwin, the secretary of treasury, is *the
Waggon-boy.* Thomas Benton, the great Missourian,
is known as *Old Bullion.* Douglas, the democratic
senator of Illinois, who is scarcely taller than Louis
Blanc or Thiers, is the *Little Giant.* General Win-
field Scott got his name of *Chippewa* from his victory
over the English in the last war, and *Hasty Plate of
Soup,* from an expression which slipt from his pen in
one of his bulletins, written hastily on the ground
where he defeated the Mexicans. General Houston,
the late President of Texas, got his name of *San
Jacinto* from the battle-field on which he had taken
prisoner the President of Mexico, Santa Anna, and
all his army. General Cass, the distinguished Senator
of Michigan, is the *Great Michigander.* Governor
William H. Seward, the most influential party leader

in the Whig ranks, is known as *Little Billy*, because he had defeated Governor Marcy in New York, by advocating the issue of smaller bills by the banks, when the democratic Marcy, true to his party principles, had vetoed the bill of the legislation in this respect.

But not only the great men, even the cities and the states have their nick-names, and they are familiar to every American. Washington for instance is *the City of magnificent distances*; New York the *Empire City*; Philadelphia the *Quaker City*; Baltimore the *Monument City*; Boston the *City of Notions*, or the *Puritan City*; Newhaven the *Elm City*; Buffalo the *Queen City of the Lakes*; Pittsburgh the *Iron City*; Cleveland the *Forest City*; Cincinnati *Porkopolis*, or the *Queen City of the West*; St. Louis the *Mound City*; Louisville the *Fall City*; New Orleans the *Crescent City*. The State of New York bearing in its arms the rising sun, with the motto, " Excelsior," is the *Empire* or *Excelsior State*; Connecticut the *Free Stone State*; Massachusetts the *Bay State*; Vermont the *Green Mountain State*; New Hampshire the *Granite State*; Rhode Island *Little Rhoda*; Pennsylvania the *Keystone State*; Virginia the *Old Dominion*, or the *Mother of States and Statesmen*; Delaware the *Diamond State*; South Carolina the *Palmetto State*; Texas the *Lone Star State*; California the *Golden Region*; Mississippi the *Bayou State*; Louisiana the *Creole State*; and Kentucky the *Dark and Bloody Ground*. The inhabitants of Florida are *Cow-*

boys; those of Ohio are called *Buckeyes;* those of Iowa *Hawkeyes;* and those of Illinois *Suckers;* the Missourians call themselves *Pukes;* the Indiana people *Hoosiers;* the Michiganians *Wulwereens;* and Wisconsinians *Badgers.* All those nicknames are familiar to, and frequently used by, the Americans, and not only in jest; in the same way as they collectively accept the designation of *Yankees,* if this word is used in contradistinction to *English.* In the States themselves the Southerners and Westerners disclaim this appellation; they use it to designate the New Englanders, whilst in New England again every State disowns it, except Connecticut, which is proud to be the original *Yankee State.*

CHAPTER III.

COLONISATION — PHYSICAL AND POLITICAL CON-
FIGURATION OF THE UNITED STATES—PARTIES,
AND THEIR SUBDIVISIONS.

I. COLONISATION.

THE question of colonisation and the establishment
of New States, so important for every statesman, is
not a new one, and the history of the colonies of
antiquity and of the middle ages, gives us the most
striking parallels with the present relations of the
great empires. The history of conquest over civilized
nations, who, after being emasculated by despotism
or internal feuds, are overrun by some more powerful
neighbour; and of the final amalgamation of conquerors and conquered,—is of course more striking,
and occupies such a prominent position in the accounts
of historians, that the slower but steadier and more
lasting progress of civilisation by the establishment
of colonies, is thrown into the background, and
scarcely noticed in our compendiums, so far that, with
the exception of the professional antiquaries and
historians, there are very few who know the difference
of principles in the establishment of the Greek, the
Roman, and the Mediæval colonies. Common to
them all is the admirable selection of site ; wherever
there is an important commercial point in Southern
Europe, in Asia Minor, and along the shores of

Northern Africa, you may be sure to find there the
ruins of ancient settlements; wherever there is an
important military position in the countries once
under the sway of the Roman Emperors, there you
find also traces of Roman camps and military establishments.

The oldest colonies we know, are Phœnician, for
the traces of Egyptian peculiarity in Athens, and
the indisputable influence of Egypt on Greece, are
not to be ascribed to colonisation, but to the superior
civilisation of some bold adventurers, or perhaps,
political refugees from the highly-cultivated Nile land,
who imparted their knowledge to the receptive
Hellenic tribes.   The forcible abduction of great
populations by the Assyrians, Babylonians and Persians, can also not be named colonisation, but even
this measure was copied as late as 1755, by the
English, who tried to transport the whole of the
French Acadians from Nova Scotia to the other
provinces, though they succeeded but partially in this
cruel and wanton attempt.   With the Phœnicians,
and after them the Greeks, the principle of colonisation, was that of complete independence to the new
settlement.   The surplus of the population, or the
discontented party defeated in the political struggles
at home, went out to seek a new home as organised
bodies, often led by an eminent noble.   As soon as they
found a place on the shores of the Mediterranean, or
the Black Sea, they established themselves there as
an independent and free commonwealth, in fact as a

republic; they gave themselves their own constitution, adopted laws, and were not bound to the mother state by any other tie, than by that same moral obligation which subsists between the parent and the son who has established his own household. They therefore were the natural allies of the mother country, they never entered into a league or war against her; they had community of religious worship and of hospitality with her, and mourned over her calamities as if they were their own. But there was, in general, no attempt made by the mother state to maintain a supremacy over the colonies, nor did the colonies ever claim the protection of the mother country as a matter of right. And under this system all the coasts of the Mediterranean, of the Euxine, and of the Chersonnese, were covered with flourishing cities, equal in wealth and commercial importance to their mother countries, able to defend themselves against the attacks of the surrounding barbarous tribes, and civilising them soon by the benefits of commercial intercourse. Miletus, though herself under Persian supremacy, became the mother of full five scores of republican colonies, and the Greek spirit had ample space and opportunity to develop itself under the most different constitutions. This system was the school in which Europe was trained, and its result is the most fragant bloom of the youth of mankind.*

* Even Fynes Clinton, in his ' Feste Hellenici,' breaks out with an admiration of the superiority of Greek colonisation over Spanish and English.

After some partial deviations from the principle of free colonies under Imperial Athens and Sparta, a general alteration took place in this system, when Philip and Alexander had established the Macedonian rule, and conquest and military glory were to replace free institutions. The Greek cities founded in the Persian Empire by Alexander and his generals, who had become kings after his death, the Alexandrias, Antiochias, Seleucias, &c. were at the same time courts and camps, the centres of Greek refinement, of Greek learning, and of an absolute administration by Greek officials; and the head-quarters of a well-disciplined army, principally composed of Greeks, and wholly officered by Greeks. The natives remained in the enjoyment of their local institutions, of their civil laws, and of their religious freedom, as long as it did not interfere with the established principles of government, which, jealous of every symptom of national independence, relied only on the army and on the spirit of materialism which it fostered among the people. It was a state of things, in some points, similar to the English rule in India, in others, to the present continental despotism.

The Roman colonies in Europe at large, originated in the camp : the head-quarters of the legions in Spain, Gaul, Germany, and England became cities; their population was at first one of soldiers, partly the regular garrison, partly veterans who were retained for exceptional service, all of them Roman citizens and living under the laws of Rome. At this time of military government useful work was not yet regarded as unbecoming to a soldier; and therefore highways and aqueducts and public monuments were raised by them. Basilicas, baths, and amphitheatres soon embellished the settlements, and villas, in which all the luxuries of Roman life were combined, in some measure comforted the commanding officers for their absence from the imperial city. But the centralising system of the Emperors drew all the moral forces of the provinces to Rome, where the life of the whole empire was concentrated; in the colonies it was as sullen as in the French colony of Algeria, which is established on the same principle.

The colonies of the middle ages are again different. They were originally commercial factories dependent entirely on the mother state, even when enlarged by the course of events into large empires. Exclusiveness and monopolies are the main features of those establishments, and therefore they were governed in the most absolute way, even when they proceeded from republics. The freedom of the mother country was never extended to the colonies, neither by Venice and Genoa,* nor by the Dutch States general; the rights of the citizens ceased across the waters. There was no self-government in the colonies, because the great bulk of the settlers were there for commercial purposes only, with the view of making money and

* Their colonies were principally along the shores of the Black Sea; Kaffa (Feodosic) was the most important of them.

of enjoying it, as soon as possible, in the mother
country, for which the colonies were but a mine of
wealth.   No attention whatever was paid to the
moral condition of the settlement; but peace was
most studiously preserved, lest the commercial interests should suffer.

The English plantations, in North America, were an
exception to the general colonial rule in the middle
ages.   The charters, granted to them, were framed on
the common basis of English local freedom, and even
under the last Stuarts, they contained more liberal
principles than those since acknowledged in England.
In fact, at that time, the government did not interfere so much with the colonists as it does now, nor
were the draughts of the charters manufactured in
Downing Street, they were often settled in the colonies themselves, and sent to London merely for the
royal sanction.   The colonists were well aware of
their own wants, and knew what kind of charters
fitted them, and they increased and prospered in
every way.   But when the centralising principles of
modern statesmenship were applied to North America,
the separation became a matter of necessity.   The
colonists would have probably consented to be governed from the banks of the Potomac, but they
knew too well that it was impossible to govern them
properly from the banks of the Thames, where their
material interests could not be known, and remained
necessarily subordinated to the imperial policy.

The same reason deprived Spain of her American

empire,* and the Braganza dynasty could not retain the imperial crown of Brazils, except under the condition of separating from Portugal, and establishing a *national administration.* The struggle which everywhere spread over the two continents of America, was not that of republican principles against monarchy, but that of local independence against foreign rule, and against the exclusion of the native Americans from all the offices of trust.† Had the royal Portuguese family not fled to the Brazils, when dethroned by Napoleon, or had King John not yielded to the demand of separation, this empire too would have become a republic, though here as well as in all Spanish America, the monarchical and Roman Catholic principles of the mother country have taken strong roots. Even the English colonies were in the beginning of the quarrel not anti-monarchical, though they have been established on the democratic principle.

It is quite remarkable to see how every attempt has failed to establish in the English colonies, social and political institutions, analogous to those at home. Bureaucracy has been extended across the oceans, the centralising tendencies of the colonial office have

* The "Plan of Iguala," the first revolutionary step in Mexico, invited the king or his brother to his American Empire.

† In Mexico this took the ecclesiastical form. The leaders of the revolt were the lower clergy, who were exasperated at all the dignities of the Church being filled by native Spaniards. Hence the intense power of the Mexican clergy in the Mexican republic, whose interests they ruin.

done enough harm to the colonies, and to the imperial finances, but to transplant the aristocratical stamp of old England, was utterly impossible; the nobility would not go into the colony, to be snubbed by bureaucrats. An upper house, consisting of nominees of the crown, such as it is established in the majority of the colonies, is a tool of centralisation, but not a nursery of aristocracy. The impossibility of making large grants of land pay rent, and perhaps the personal vanity of the English nobility, stood in the way of establishing a colonial hereditary nobility, local peers, who, in England, would have been lords without a seat in the Imperial Parliament, like the Irish or Scotch peers. Now it is too late for such a measure, which perhaps would have preserved the American States to the British Empire; and there cannot be any doubt that, when the ties between the Colonies and England shall be loosened, and in the course of time entirely dissolved, all those new States will be constituted without an aristocracy and without an established church, on the same basis as the United States.

In the North American republic colonisation and the foundation of new States presents now no difficulties whatever;—there is no longer any problem to be solved. As long as the settlers in a new territory are too few to be able to establish a regular administration, the general government determines the boundaries of the territory, sends judges to it, and names the governor and his officials from amongst the

settlers, who, in their turn, send a delegate to Congress, to represent their interests. As soon as their
number increases, and their resources are somewhat
developed, Congress authorises them to meet, by their
elected delegates,* in convention, they adopt a constitution, and request that they may be admitted into the
Union, which, provided that the constitution is republican, and consistent in its main features with the
principles of the constitution of the United States, is
always agreed to; and by admission into the Union
each State gets its perfect sovereignty. The general
Government has no desire to introduce uniformity
in the constitutions, or the criminal or civil laws of
the new States; the aristocracy of the South, the
democracy of the West and North, and even the
theocratical forms of the Mormons, in the territory
of Utah, are not interfered with. The old States
alter their constitution without difficulty or excitement, and every theory of legislation has a chance
of being adopted, as an experiment, in one or
other State. The United States are thus an unbounded field on which the energies of the spirit
of mankind can easily develop themselves, unfettered
by the traditions of the past and the fears of the
future; and, since their separation from England,
have enlarged themselves to an extent wholly unprecedented.

The progress of American civilization towards the
west, has, as it seems, a normal law of growth. " Up

* This is virtually the history of Virginia under James.

to the year 1840," says Colonel Gilpin,* "the progress, whereby seventy-six States and four territories had been established and peopled, had amounted to a solid strip of twenty-five miles in depth, added *annually* along the western face of the Union from Canada to the Gulf. This occupation of wild territory, accumulating outward like the annual rings of the forest-trees, proceeds with all the solemnity of a providential ordinance. It is at this moment sweeping onward to the Pacific, with accelerated activity and force, like a deluge of men, rising unabatedly, and daily pushed onward by the hand of God. It is from the statistics accumulated in the bureaus at Washington, the decimal census, sales of public lands, and assessments of state and national taxes, that we deduce with certainty the law of this deluge of human beings, which nothing interrupts and no power can stop. Fronting the Union on every side is a great army of pioneers. This vast body, numbering 500,000 at least, has the movements and obeys the discipline of a perfectly organized military force. It is every moment recruited by individuals, by families, and, in some instances, by communities, from every village, county, city, and state in the Union, and by emigrants from other nations. Each man in this moving throng is in force a platoon. He makes a farm upon the outer edge of the settlements, which he occupies for a year, and then sells to the leading files of the mass pressing

* In a speech delivered in St. Louis, at a meeting in 1851.

up to him from behind. He again advances twenty-five miles, renews his farm, is again overtaken, and again sells. As individuals fall out from the front rank, or fix themselves permanently, others rush from behind, pass to the front, and assail the wilderness in their turn."

What has been the result? Another western man, Mr. Drake, answers:—"Sixty-two years ago, in 1790, the centre of population was twenty-two miles *east* of Washington city. In a single decade, we find the centre in 1800 to be thirty miles *west* of Washington; in 1820 it was seventy-one miles west of Washington; in 1830, one hundred and eight miles; in 1840, one hundred and sixty; and 1850, it had crossed the Alleghany, and was planted down in the young state of Ohio."

" Previous to the late war with Mexico," continues Colonel Gilpin, " this busy throng of pioneers was engaged at one point in occupying the peninsula of Florida, and the land secured by emigrant Indian tribes; at another in reaching the copper region of Lake Superior, and in absorbing Iowa and Wisconsin. From Missouri had gone forth a forlorn hope, to occupy Oregon and California; Texas was thus annexed, the Indian country pressed upon its flanks, and spy-companies reconnoitering New and Old Mexico. Even then, obeying that mysterious and uncontrollable impulse which drives the American nation to its goal, a body of the hardiest race that ever faced varied and unnumbered privations and dangers, embarked upon the track to the Pacific coast, forced their way to the end, encountering and defying dangers and difficulties unparalleled, with a courage and success, the like to which the world has rarely seen. Thus, then, overland sweeps this tide-wave of population, absorbing in its thundering march the glebe, the savages, and the wild beasts of the wilderness, scaling the mountains and debouching down upon the seaboard. Upon the Atlantic sea-coast, of high latitude, the pioneer force has thrown itself into ships, and found in the ocean fishery food for its creative genius. The whaling fleet is the *marine force* of the pioneers army. These two forces by land and sea, have both worked steadily onward to the North Pacific. They now re-unite in the harbours of Oregon and California, about to bring into existence upon the Pacific, a commercial grandeur, identical with that which has followed them upon the Atlantic.

" National wars stimulate progress, for in those periods of excitement, the adventurous brush through the cobweb-laws spun by the metaphysics of peace. Then it is that the young pioneers, entering the armies of the frontier, rush out and reconnoitre the unpruned wilderness. During the revolution, little armies, issuing down the Alleghanies, passed over Kentucky, Tennessee, and the North-Western Territory. These new countries were reconnoitred and admired. With hardy frames, confirmed health, and recruited by a year or two of peace, these soldiers returned to occupy the choice spots which had been their bivouac and their camping grounds. From the campaigns of war grew the settlements of peace, and populous states displaced the wilderness. Another war came with another generation; armies penetrated into Michigan, Upper Illinois, and through Mississippi. The great Mississippi river, crossed at many points, ceased to be a barrier, and the steam-boat appeared ploughing its yellow flood. Five great states, five territories, and three millions of people now emblazon its western side!

" And now again has come another generation and another war. The American armies have scaled the icy barriers of the ' mother mountain,' and the (Mexican) Andes. Hidden for a time in the mazes of their manifold peaks and ridges, they have issued out at many points upon the beach of the blue Pacific. Passing round by the great oceans, a military marine simultaneously strikes the shore, and lends them aid. Thus is the wilderness reconnoitred in war, its geography illustrated, and its conquerors disciplined. The young soldiers, resting for a moment at home, resuming the civil wreath and weapons of husbandry, have sallied forth again, to give to the country great roads of commerce, and a sisterhood of maritime states on the new found ocean. Only a few years ago, the nation, misled by prejudices, regarded the great western worlds uninhabitable, and the new ocean out of reach. War came, a hundred thousand soldiers and as many citizens went forth, penetrated everywhere, and returned to relate in every open ear, the wonderful excellence of the climates and countries they had seen.   Hence have come already those new states on this other sea board, and the renewed vivacity of progress with which the general heart now palpitates. Will this cease or slacken? Has the pouring forth of the stream from Europe ever ceased since the day of Columbus? Has the grass obliterated the trails down the Alleghanies, or across the Mississippi? Rather let him who doubts, seat himself upon the bank of our magnificent river and await the running day of its yellow waters, for sooner shall he see this, than a cessation in the crowd now flowing loose to the western seaboard! Gold is dug; lumber is manufactured; pastoral and arable agriculture grow apace; a marine flashes into existence; commerce resounds; the fisheries are prosecuted; vessels are built; steam pants through all the waters. Each interest stimulating all the rest, and perpetually creating novelties, a career is commenced, to which, as it glances across the Pacific, the human eye assigns no term."

This glowing description of American colonisation, by a man who himself belongs to the first explorers of the overland route and of the Rocky Mountains, and who took part in the war against Mexico, is likewise a specimen of western eloquence, and bears the stamp of the energy which pervades those pioneers of civilisation whom he describes.

But the way and progress of colonisation in America

has been prefigured and determined by the physical configuration of the Western continent, which arrests the attention of the philosophical observer by its peculiarity.

II. PHYSICAL CONFIGURATION OF NORTH AMERICA.

By her natural configuration, America is entirely different from the old continent. In central Europe the principal chains of mountains, as the Pyrenees, the Alps, Carpathians, and the Balkan, run east and west, forming walls against the northern winds, and the many other intersecting ranges which radiate from the central trunk in other directions, divide the continent into many water-basins, each different in its principal features. On the contrary, all the mountain ranges of North America—as, first, the White and Green Mountains, the Catskills, Alleghanies, and Apalachians, which form the eastern mountain range; next the central Sierra Madre (Rocky Mountains), and then the western range of the Nevada—run in a south-northern direction, dividing the country into four unequal parts: the eastern sea-coast, bordered by the Atlantic and the Alleghanies; the great Mississippi Basin,* up to the Rocky Mountains; the table-lands included between them and the Snowy Mountains, and the sloping sea-coast of the Pacific. The cold northern winds from the

* The Americans say always the Mississippi valley, whilst it would be more correct to call it the basin of the Mississippi.

Pole sweep occasionally through the two former of
these valleys, and so do the warm breezes of the
Mexican Gulf, making the temperature colder in
winter and hotter in summer, and altogether more
variable than in Europe.

The eastern sea-coast is the smallest but the most
renowned of these natural subdivisions of America; it
contains the old thirteen original States, with their
merchant and planter population, and commercial
interest. Less than one-half of the Mississippi valley
is occupied by the western agricultural States, which,
by and by, will multiply and extend up to the table-
land. The woodless dry table-land, with its poorer
soil, rich only in coals and salt, is destined to be
peopled by shepherds, forming here a succession of
pastoral States, whilst Oregon and California combine
the agricultural, mining, and commercial interests of
the eastern shore, and of the great west.

Colonel Gilpin, a man whose comprehensive mind,
and indomitable energy, may yet give him an important place in his country, describes the natural
features of North America in the following very
graphic way—surveying first the basaltic formation
from the Rocky Mountains to the Pacific, and then
the calcareous Atlantic region.*

"The chain of the Andes, debouching north from
the Isthmus, opens like the letter Y, into two primary

---

* The reader will excuse the lengthy quotation; but the subject
has not yet been treated sufficiently, and the views of a man, who
had formed them on the spot, deserve attention so much the more
as they are given in an attractive form.

chains, or Cordilleras. On the right the Sierra
Madre (Rocky Mountains), with their *Piedmont,* the
Black Hills, which mask the front of the Sierra,
trending along the coast of the Mexican Gulf, divides
the Northern Continent almost centrally,* forming
an unbroken water-shed to Behring's Straits. On
the left the Andes follow the coast of the Pacific,
warp around the Gulf of California, and passing along
the coast of California and Oregon, under the name
of Sierra Nevada, terminates also near Behring Straits.
The immense interval between these chains is a
succession of intramontane basins, and forms the
great platform of table-lands. The two first of these
basins, in the territory of the republic of Mexico,
have no outlet to either ocean, and their waters are
dispersed by evaporation; the third is the Basin del
Norte, whose vast area feeds the Rio del Norte, the
Conchos, and Pechos. These, concentrated into the
Rio Grande, have by their united volume, burst
through the outer wall of the Sierra, and found an
outlet towards the Atlantic. The next, the Basin of
the Great Colorado of the West,—the most unknown
part of the United States, embraces *above* the great
rivers Rio Verde and Rio Grande, whose confluent
waters, penetrating the mighty Cordillera of the
Andes athwart from base to base, discharge them-

* Colonel Gilpin takes the Black Hills for a Piedmont of the
Rocky Mountains,—a plateau rent and torn by the fissures of innumerable streams. Taking this view, he is correct in his statement;
the Black Hills being nearly at equal distances from New York and
San Francisco.

selves into the Gulf of California. Into this sublime
gorge, the *Cannon of the Colorado*, the human eye
has never swept for an interval of 375 miles. After
this, the basin of the Great Salt Lake, like the
Caspian of Asia, containing many small basins within
one great, and losing its scattered waters by evaporation, has no outflow to either ocean. The sixth is
the Basin of the Columbia, lying across the northern
flanks of the two last, grand above them all in position and configuration. Many great rivers, besides
the Snake and Upper Columbia, descending from the
great arc of the Sierra Madre, where it circles towards
the north-west, from the 43d to the 52d degree,
concentrate above the *Cascades,* into a single trunk,
which strikes here the mighty Cordillera of the Andes,
narrowed to one ridge, and disgorges itself through
this pass into the open Pacific. It is here, descending
by the grade of this river, from the rim of the Valley
of the Mississippi, that the great débouché of the
American Continent towards the West is formed, and
here will be the pathway of future generations, as
the people of the Old World pass down the Mediterranean, and out by Gibraltar. Above, the basin
of Frazer River forms a seventh table-land, and sends
its waters through the Andes to the Pacific.

"With the geography of the more northern region
we are imperfectly acquainted, knowing however that
from Pugett's Sound to Behring Straits the wall of
the Andes forms the beach itself of the Pacific, whilst
the Sierra Madre forms the western rim of the basins

of the Saskatchewan of the Hudson Bay, and of the
Mac Kenzie of the Arctic Seas. Thus then briefly
we arrive at the cardinal department of the geography
of the continent, viz., the table-lands—being a longi-
tudinal section about two-sevenths of the whole
area intermediate between the two oceans, but walled
from both, and having but three outlets for its waters,
the Rio Grande, the Colorado, and Columbia.

" Columnar basalt forms the basement of this whole
region, and volcanic action is everywhere prominent.
Its general level is about 6000 feet above the sea.
Rain seldom falls, and timber is rare. The ranges
of mountains which separate the basins are often
rugged and capped with perpetual snow, whilst
isolated masses of great height elevate themselves
from the plains. Such is the region of the table-
lands; beyond these is the maritime region, for the
great wall of the Andes, receding from the beach of
the Pacific, leaves between itself and the sea a half
valley, as it were, forming the seaboard slope, across
which descends to the sea a series of fine rivers, like
the little streams descending from the Alleghanies
to the Atlantic. This resembles and balances the
maritime slope of the Atlantic side of the continent,
from the Alleghanies to the sea; it is of the highest
agricultural excellence, basaltic in formation, and
grand beyond the powers of description, the snowy
points of the Andes being everywhere visible from
the sea, whilst its climate is entirely exempt from
the frosts of winter.

" Such, and so grand, is our continent towards the
Pacific.   Let us turn our glance towards the Atlantic
and Arctic Oceans, and scan the geography in our
front.   *Four* great valleys appear, each one drained
by a river of first magnitude.   First, the Mississippi
valley, greatest in magnitude, and embracing the
heart and splendour of the continent, gathers the
waters of 1,500,000 square miles, and sheds them
into the Gulf of Mexico; second, the St. Lawrence,
whose river flows into the North Atlantic; third,
the Nelson and Severn Rivers into the Hudson's
Bay; and fourth, the great valley of the Mac Kenzie
River, rushing north into the Hyperborean Sea.
These valleys, everywhere calcareous, have a uniform surface, gently rolling, but destitute of mountains, and pass into one another by dividing ridges,
which distribute their own waters into each valley,
but whose superior elevation is only distinguishable
among the general undulations by the water-sheds
they form.   Around the whole continent, leaving a
comparatively narrow slope towards the oceans, runs
a rim of mountains, giving the idea of a vast amphi-
theatre.   Through this rim penetrate, towards the
south-east and north, the above great rivers only,
forming at their débouchés the natural doors of the
interior; but no stream penetrates west, through the
Sierra Madre, which forms an unbroken water-shed
from the Isthmus to Behring Straits.   Thus we find
more than three-fifths of our continent to consist of
a limitless plain, intersected by countless navigable

streams, flowing everywhere from the circumference towards common centres grouped in close proximity, and only divided by what connects them into one homogeneous plan.

" To the American people, then, belongs this vast interior space, covered over its uniform surface of 2,300,000 square miles with the richest calcareous soil, touching the snows towards the north, and the torrid heats towards the south, bound together by an infinite internal navigation, of a temperate climate, and constituting in the whole the most magnificent dwelling-place marked out by God for man's abode.

" There we perceive in the formation of the Atlantic part of the American Continent, a sublime simplicity, a complete economy of arrangement singular to itself, and the reverse of what distinguishes the ancient world. To understand this, let us compare them.

" Europe, the smallest of the grand divisions of the land, contains in its centre the icy masses of the Alps; from around their declivities radiate the large rivers of that continent, the Danube directly east to the Euxine, the Po south-east to the Adriatic, the Rhone south-west to the Mediterranean, the Rhine to the Northern Ocean. Walled off by the Pyrenees, and Carpathians, and the Ural, divergent and isolated are the Tagus, the Elbe, the Vistula, the Don, and Volga, and other single rivers, affluents of the Baltic, of the Atlantic, of the Mediterranean, and of the Euxine. Descending from common radiant points, and diverging every way from one another, no intercommunication exists between the rivers of Europe; navigation is petty and feeble, nor have art and commerce, during many centuries, united so many small valleys, remotely isolated by impenetrable barriers. Hence upon each river dwells a distinct people, different from all the rest in race, language, habits, and interests. Though often politically amalgamated by conquest, they again relapse into fragments from innate geographical incoherence. The history of these nations is a story of perpetual war.

"Exactly similar to Europe, though grander in size and populations, is Asia. From the stupendous central barrier of the Himalaya and the table-land of Tartary run the great rivers of China,* the Blue and the Yellow, due east to discharge themselves beneath the rising sun; towards the south runs the rivers of India, the Indus and Ganges, with their tributaries; towards the west, the Oxus and Jaxartes; and north to the Arctic Seas, the four great rivers of Siberia. During fifty centuries, as now, the Alps and the Hindukush have proved inseparable barriers to the amalgamation of nations around their bases, and dwelling in the valleys which radiate from their slopes. The continent of Africa, as far as we know

---

* The rivers of China are comparable to the Mississippi. China is a large empire, a world in itself, yet her natural configuration, similar to the Mississippi valley and the adjoining country, led to centralisation and stagnation. Europe resisted this for a long time, by the very peculiarity marked as undesirable by Colonel Gilpin; he seems to have sympathy with centralisation.

the details of its surface, is even more than these split into disjointed fragments.

"Thus the continents of the Old World resemble a bowl placed bottom upwards, which scatters everything poured upon it, whilst Northern America, right side up, receives and gathers towards its centre whatever falls within its rim.

"Behold then the future of America graven in the geographical lines and arteries of her symmetrical ocean-bound expanse! Behold it foretold in the oracular prophecies of past and present progress.

"America, in geography the antithesis of the Old World, will remain the same in society. Our country will rapidly attain to a population equalling that of the rest of the world combined, forming a single people, identical in manners, language, customs, and impulses, preserving the same civilisation, imbued with the same opinions, and having the same political liberties. Of this we have two illustrations now under our eye, the one passing away, the other advancing. The aboriginal Indian race, amongst whom, from Darien to the Esquimaux, and from Florida to Vancouver's Island, exists a perfect identity in their hair, complexion, features, stature, and language ;* and second, in the instinctive fusion into one language, and one new race of immigrant

* Colonel Gilpin goes too far in this respect; they belong to the same race; they are all beardless, but the colour of their hair, skin, and eyes varies. The language, too, belongs to the same stock, but no two tribes can understand each other.

Germans, English, Irish, French, and Spanish, whose
individualities are obliterated in a single generation.

" Climate distinctly controls the migrations of the
human race, which has steadily adhered to an isothermal line around the world. The extremely mild
climate of our Western seaboard is only the consequence of the same great laws of nature which
operate in Western Europe. These are the regular
and fixed ordinances of the code of nature, to which
the migrations of man, in common with the animal,
yield an instinctive obedience. Within the torrid zone
and up to 30 degrees of the northern hemisphere blow
the trade winds, and ' variables' constantly from the
east and north-east all around the world, but the upper
halves of the elliptical orbits followed by the winds, lie
in the temperate zone, from 35 to 60 degrees, within
which the winds flow constantly from the west to south-
west. These winds reach the western coasts of America
and Europe, after traversing the expanse of the Pacific
and Atlantic Oceans. Warmed to the same temperature as these oceans, they impart again this same mild
atmosphere to the maritime fronts of the continent
which receive them. These same winds passing onward
over great extensions of continent of low temperature,
covered with snow and frozen during winter, often
warped upward by mountain ranges, becoming exhausted of their warmth, have upon the eastern portion
of both hemispheres an exactly opposite effect upon
the climate. Hence the different temperature of New
York and Lisbon, which face one another on the

opposite coasts of the Atlantic—of Pekin and San Francisco, similiarly opposite on the Pacific. At San Francisco and Lisbon the seasons are but modulations of one continuous summer, at New York and Pekin winter suspends vegetation during six months, whilst ice and snow bridge the land and waters. These four cities are all close upon the same parallel of latitude, the 40th degree."

It is remarkable that the largest number of important cities are situated under about the same latitude, between 39 to 41 degrees—Pekin and Samarkand, Constantinople and Naples, Madrid and Lisbon, New York and San Francisco. "It is within a belt of the earth straddling the 40th degree of north latitude," says Col. Gilpin, "that the greatest mass of land surrounds the world, and where the continents most nearly approach. Within this belt, from 30 to 50 degrees, four-fifths of the human race is assembled, and here the civilised nations, of whom we possess any history, have succeeded one another, commencing at the farthest extremity of Asia and forming a zodiac towards the setting sun. This succession has flowed onward in an even course, undulating along an isothermal line, until in our time the ring is about to close around the earth's circumference by the arrival of the American nation on the coast of the Pacific, which looks over on Asia.

" It is here manifest how in Asia the masses of populations lie below the 40th degree, in Europe above, and again so far in America, curving downward on the eastern face of our continent, to rise again to the north upon the warm coast of the Pacific. Thus has the zodiac of nations, our own nation similarly with the rest, pursued a serpentine line of equal temperature, retaining all around the world similar employments, similar industrial pursuits, similar food and clothing, requiring similarity of climate, and recoiling alike from the Torrid and the Arctic Zone."

It is a well known fact, that civilisation is the result of frequent intercourse of different nations, and of the exchange of ideas and experiences between them. The sea therefore, the great pathway of commerce and intercourse, has always been the great civilizer of mankind. The coasts of the Mediterranean have been the cradle of science and of religions, the starting point for progress in antiquity; and the islands, the deep bays, and inlets of Greece, which brought commerce into the centre of the Peninsula, made this happily articulated country the centre of ancient civilisation. The great navigable rivers had a similar effect on mankind by the same reasons, and the outlet of the Yellow and Blue Rivers, of the Ganges and Indus, of the Euphrates and of the Nile, were similar centres of commerce, wealth, arts, and science, whilst the rigid forms of the coast of Africa, without deep bays, and great navigable rivers, without a chain of islands around it, without protruding peninsulas,—bridges for commercial intercourse,—has remained until now a barren barbarous wilderness, obstructing all progress by its natural configuration.

Russia, too, has an unfavourable position, her greatest
rivers run towards the inhospitable Arctic Seas,
bound by barriers of ice, and the Wolga disgorges
his magnificent waters into an Inland Sea, without
ebb and flood and an outlet. Her commerce and
people, curtailed by nature of the cheapest means of
locomotion, must remain stationary, with the exception of the basin of the Don and Dnieper, and the
shores of Crimæa and the Euxine, the country of
the Cossacks, who likewise are in every respect a
superior race to the Moscovites. But as well as
politically, the United States are also geographically
the reverse of Russia, and their water communications
surpass even those of Southern and Western Europe.
On their Eastern boundaries, the great Massachusetts
Bay, the estuary of New York, the Delaware, and
Chesapeak Bay, are destined by nature to be the
seats of commerce and civilized art; on their northern
frontier the series of the mighty soft water lakes,
the Ontario, Erie, Huron, Michigan, and Superior,
has become a natural pathway of commercial intercourse, deeply extending into the heart of the
continent, in importance for mankind, second only
to the Mediterranean Sea, and like this, surrounded
by a garland of flourishing cities. But the most
important feature of these lakes, is the absence of
any mountain range to divide them, either from the
Atlantic or from the basin of the Mississippi; short
canals have connected the waters of the Erie on one
side with the Hudson, and by this river with New

York Bay ; on the other with the Ohio, Mississippi, and Gulf of Mexico. Other canals partly constructed, partly in construction, lead the waters of the Ontario down to the Hudson, and those of the Michigan by the Wabash to the Ohio; the watershed between the lakes and the great valley of the Mississippi is imperceptible, and everywhere easily surmounted without extraordinary means of engineering.

But the most important feature of American hydrography is the Mississippi itself. This immense river, rather connected with, than separated from, the basin of the lakes, runs from the forty-seventh degree north, along almost the same meridian of longitude,— a course of 2600 miles, till it discharges itself into the Gulf of Mexico, receiving in its course the waters of innumerable tributaries. The waters of the Alleghanies are carried down by the beautiful Ohio and its tributaries the Kanawha, Cumberland, and Tennessee; the Rocky Mountains send their waters by the mighty Missouri, the Arkansas, and the Red River. Messengers from the four quarters of the continent, to use the poetical words of Mr. Charles D. Drake, they bear their watery burdens to cast into the channel, through which flows the rushing flood of the father of waters, which, in its course of 2000 miles, from the Falls of St. Antony to Balize, receives the waters of 10,000 miles of direct tributaries, of which 5000 miles are navigable,—and those of 8000 miles of indirect tributaries, of which again 5000 are known to be navi-

gable, but the future will doubtless show that that
computation falls far short of the reality. We are,
therefore, safe in saying, that this flood and its
tributaries, direct and indirect, amount to at least
13,000 miles of navigable waters, a net of natural
communications over eighteen States and three territories. An area of 800,000 square miles, and eleven
and a half millions of people, are directly connected
with, and interested in, this great stream,—more than
half of the States of the Union, more than half of its
organised territories; and about half of its people.
Five of those States belong to the original thirteen,
to the Atlantic commercial sea-coast States; and
again seven are planter States, and six agricultural
free States. All the different interests of the Union
are connected with the Mississippi, which, therefore,
by its tributaries, and the canals which connect it
with the lakes and the East, becomes the most important tie of the Union, fastening the south to the
north, and the east to the west. By the connection
of the Ohio with Lake Erie, and of Lake Erie with
the Hudson, it has become the great artery of North
America, which carries life through all its limbs, the
great channel of inland commerce with the two
outlets, New York and New Orleans, and the great
commercial cities of Pittsburg, Wheeling, Cincinnati,
Louisville, and St. Louis, along the banks. " Place
yourself, in imagination," says Mr. Drake, " at the
mouth of our river, and look at it and its tributaries
on the map of this continent. See how like a mighty

tree it stands, its head towering up nearly to the frigid zone,* its roots striking down nearly to the tropic, its giant branches stretching far and wide over the land from east to west, embowering beneath their dense and refreshing shade millions of freemen, united in interest, in government, in language, and in destiny. There it stands, inviting the oppressed of all nations to take refuge under its verdure, while its grateful odours float over the world, arousing the nations that groan under despotism to a sense of their rights, and inspiring them with courage to assert and maintain them."

Such are the principal natural features of the immense country which acknowledges the constitution of the United States as her organic law, so entirely different in the main features from the constitutions of Europe.†

III. POLITICAL CONFIGURATION OF THE UNITED STATES.

Before the fifteenth, sixteenth, and even eighteenth centuries, the nations of Europe differed much more in respect to the forms of government than now. Though nearly all of them were constitutional, the checks and balances were different in every country, according to the requirements of the people and its

---

* Pembina, the farthest settlement in Michigan towards the north, has, under 49 degrees northern latitude, a Siberian climate.

† 'The Mission of the Mississippi.' A speech delivered by Mr. Drake, at St. Louis.

historical development. But the intermarriages and the standing armies of the princes in all the great realms of Europe, swept those constitutional restraints away in the short space of a century. England was the only country which did not lose, but strengthened, her free institutions in the struggle between the Crown and the Parliament; and as her power and wealth increased rapidly, whilst the despotically ruled nations lost their former influence soon after the overthrow of their freedom, England was held up by the philosophers of the eighteenth century as the prototype of a constitutional monarchy. Therefore, when, during and since the great French Revolution, constitutions were devised for the different nations of Europe, they were always shaped, or at least said to be shaped, according to the English model,* though it is fully understood that the English aristocracy is peculiar to the English, and that this institution, and the aristocratic spirit and legislature in respect to landed property, does not, and cannot exist anywhere on the continent. The study of public law has by this means become very much abridged, and the word constitution got a quite conventional meaning amongst the journalists, and professional politicians, viz., a combination of a King and a Parliament consisting

* This was the case in France in 1789, 1815, and 1830; in Portugal, in Spain, in Belgium, in Holland, in Piedmont, in Greece, in the different German States, in Sicily, and in Naples for the short time it had a constitution. Norway, Sweden, and Switzerland, are the only exceptions at the present time, their constitution bearing no internal affinity with the English.

of Peers and Commons. The result of this combination in England was, that the Crown in conjunction
with the Parliament destroyed, little by little, the
municipal life, and introduced the uniformity of centralisation; that on the other side, the Parliament,
backed by the masses, curtailed the traditional pre-
rogative of the Crown, until at length *parliamentary
omnipotence* was established, the representatives of a
portion of the nation and the hereditary peers exer-
cising the most unlimited legislative power, leaving
for the Crown but the theoretical right of the veto,
the choice of the ministry from amongst one of the
two aristocratic parties of the Parliament, and the
dissolution of the latter. Towards the nation, Parliament is yet less checked. The member has in fact, to
give a palatable speech to his constituency before his
election; but, generally speaking, he has not much to
care for the opinion of the electors. He can absent
himself at every important occasion, and he may
vote against the wishes of his constituents, for he
cannot be called to account; not to mention the
inequality of the constituencies, which are so arranged
as to give in every case a large majority of the seats
in the House of Commons to the aristocracy of the
country. Theoretically, it is a very illogical consti-
stution, but practically, it works reasonably enough,
because it does not obstruct the development of the
nation, whose mind is sound, and whose character is
sober and moral; and therefore even the faults of
the constitution become of value, as there is always

something to be mended, and the great community can rejoice every year that their matchless constitution has again been improved.

For the Continent, the combination of King, Peers, and Commons, has a somewhat different meaning, according to the notions even of the English liberal newspapers and statesmen. In England, it means parliamentary omnipotence; on the Continent merely the omnipotence of the Crown, under the screen of legislative forms. In England, the government must retire, if defeated in the Commons after the appeal to the people by a dissolution, and the Crown must take its advisers from the opposition. On the Continent, on the contrary, the Commons must submit after a dissolution, lest the Crown declares that "it is impossible to go on with this constitution," and abolishes it altogether, rather than to give up an un-popular minister or measure. The philosophy of English constitutionalism is evidently, that the government and the majority of Parliament must be of the same principles; if there arises a difference of opinions between them, the one of the two must yield, otherwise it would be impossible to avoid either a revolution or a *coup d'état*.

According to this theory, all the European journals predicted the French catastrophe long before it hap-pened. The constitution of 1848 was criticised most severely for establishing two supreme powers—one legislative, the other executive—both responsible to the people, but neither of them so far superior to the other as to have the means of forcing the other to give way. The President not having the power of dissolving the Assembly, an eventual collision could have no termination but in a revolution or a coup d'état, in order to prevent a standstill of the administration. The leading English journals were not at all averse to the principle of the latter. Had Louis Bonaparte reestablished liberty in some other form, and without wanton ferocity, they would have forgotten the perjury inherent in a coup d'état, and easily pardoned it; it was his slaughters, his proscriptions, deportations, confiscations, and the restriction of the press, which aroused the English papers in battle array against the successful usurper.

It was but a few days after the arrival of the tidings about the 2d of December, that I came to Washington, under the impression of the coup d'état, and of all the previous diatribes on the inevitable consequences of a collision between the executive power and the Legislative Assembly, which, in all the papers of Europe, preceded the tragedy of Paris. But when I inquired about the constitution of the land and the party statistics in Washington, I found, to my great astonishment, two supreme powers established, both issuing from the universal suffrage of the nation, the executive and the legislative, the President not having the power of dissolving the Congress; and actually, I found a Whig President, surrounded by a Whig ministry, whilst the Whigs were in a considerable minority in the Senate as well as in the Assembly, and yet nobody seemed to be afraid either of a revolution or of a coup d'état, or of a standstill of the administration. The reason is, that neither the President nor the Congress has anything to do with the government of the individual States, which govern themselves as sovereign States. The executive and Congress have but the general direction of the Union, not its government, in the European sense of the word. The President has no nomination, nor any share whatever in the election of the officials of any State, nor has the Congress the power to interfere with the way in which the administration and legislation of the individual States is going on.

I saw, at once the difference of the basis of the constitution in America and Europe: in America they do not know anything about parliamentary omnipotence; in Europe, nothing about the inviolability of municipal autonomy, developed in America as State rights. I had later often the opportunity to see how the constitution of the United States leaves perfect freedom to each State, and how this admirable arrangement suits the wants of a country whose climate, population, and interests are so much at variance, and which occupies the whole extent of a continent from 28 to 49 degrees north latitude. The freedom and sovereignty guaranteed by the constitution to the individual States gives to the Union so sound and broad a basis, that all the alarm about its dissolution, which excites the people at certain intervals, turns out to be void of any serious foundation. And yet this constitution was framed at a time when the Union comprised merely the eastern sea-shore States, and had scarcely extended over the Alleghanies ! Even the boldest statesman amongst the framers of the constitution could not anticipate that their work was to be recognised as the organic law over the whole temperate zone of North America. There is something providential in this most important social arrangement.

Never did the Americans aim at a uniformity like the French, or even like the English; never at concentrating the legislative power in the Congress; each State's legislature makes and unmakes the civil and criminal laws for the State. They contract debts and tax themselves as they please; they regulate their banking system and financial administration; they provide for the education. Each State has its own full sovereignty, with the exception of a few powers ceded to the general government. They gave up the right to enter into any treaty, alliance, or confederation with another State or foreign power, or engage in war, coin money, or lay duty on imports, exports, or tonnage.—To pass any bill of attainder, ex post facto law, or law impairing the obligation of contracts, or grant any title of nobility, to make a law respecting an establishment of religion, or prohibiting the free exercise thereof, or abridging freedom of speech, or of the press, or the right of the people peaceably to assemble and to petition the government for a redress of grievances;—all these points are forbidden to each State, as well as to the Congress of the Union. The right of the people to bear arms cannot be infringed by Congress, and the trial by jury is secured to every person.

So far, and not farther, has the sovereignty of the States been curtailed by their own assent, and the latitude which each of them retained for the expansion and free action of the spirit of the people, has produced a different development of the nation in the different groups of States. In fact, if we analyse the character of the people in the different parts of the Union, we shall find that there are four great republics in the United States, four great groups of States combined in the Union, each of them of a peculiar national stamp: New England, the Middle States, the South, and the West.

1. New England comprises the States of Maine, Massachusetts, New Hampshire, Rhode Island, Connecticut, and Vermont, peopled by the descendants of the Puritans of Massachusetts Bay, by the sons of the Pilgrim Fathers of Plymouth Rock. It is as classical a land of liberty as Marathon or Thermopylæ. It is the home of the free-schools—an educational system utterly unconnected with the church, which puts science within the reach of every individual without exception; it is the country of the manufacturers, of the fishers at Newfoundland, of the whalers of the Arctic and Antarctic. The citizens of New England, and especially those of Massachusetts, Connecticut, and Maine, have retained something of

the character of their ancestors, who did not consider
themselves as subject to any laws, excepting those of
reason, equity, and scripture, and had modelled their
government originally according to their own pleasure.   They are hitherto the freest commonwealth
on earth, all their towns and cities being so many
republics, taxing and governing themselves in their
primary meetings.   The cold, puritanic aversion to
all public enjoyment which is not principally intellectual, the deepest religious feeling without any
intolerance (though mingled with some instinctive
repugnance against Roman Catholicism), industry,
temperance, sobriety, and earnestness of purpose—
are features characteristic of them.   But there is also
a lack of imagination among them, and the onesided
development of the mere understanding has made
them the shrewdest people on earth, always eager for
getting information and money.   It is especially here
that public opinion does not endure anybody whose
life has no specific aim; everybody must work; he
must make or lose money; society does not tolerate
an idle life of enjoyment.   In Europe, a contemplative
life without cares, a secure income and its undisturbed
enjoyment, the " otium cum dignitate" of the Roman,
is too often the aim of life, and any other employment
than war or government is thought unbecoming for the
aristocracy.   In New England the curse of the Lord,
that " Man shall eat bread in the sweat of his face,"
has been turned into blessing; to work is an honour,
and no kind of work or labour dishonours.   It is

difficult to explain to the New Englander how it comes to pass, that a lawyer or a banker may become a lord in England, whilst no lord ever can become, or even remain a lawyer or a banker. The nucleus of the aristocracy in Europe is derived from the chiefs who swayed over hosts of serfs, working for, and ruled and protected by them; the democratic society of New England was established on the ground of equality and labour. Their soil is poor, but their schools and colleges are superior to those of the rest of the Union, and wealth and intelligence have been diffused all over New England. There is no ragged person, no decaying cottage to be seen; three-fourths of the teachers in the schools of North America are New Englanders, and whenever you see a rising commercial city, or a flourishing manufacturing establishment in the West or South, you will find also a strong infusion of New England blood.

2. The Middle States—New York, Pennsylvania, Maryland, Ohio, and, by her geographical position, New Jersey, are the seat of the great commercial interests, represented by the cities New York, Philadelphia, Baltimore, and Cincinnati. Their population was originally less homogeneous than in New England, for every part of Great Britain and Ireland, the Netherlands, all Germany, and Sweden, have furnished their quota to the formation of this new people, whose character is excitable in politics, lively in society, gambling in speculation. Their cities, their press, their politics, are not provincial but

imperial; their exchanges rule over the markets, their banks regulate the paper-currency all over the other States, and their vote decides the election of the President. It is the country of bold politicians, of adventurous speculators, of colossal fortunes and reverses. Easily carried away by sudden enthusiasm, and readier to promise than to fulfil, the people of the Middle States seem fickle; and if the calculating inquisitiveness of New England becomes sometimes tedious, the natural pride of the Middle States, mingled often with vain boasting, is equally disagreeable to the foreigner. But their comprehensive mind— which teaches them to consider more the general interests of the Union, than the particular policy of the State, and sometimes even of the party—gives the direction of the affairs of the United States into their hands. It is they who keep the balance of power between the stubborn New England, the hot-blooded South, and the young West; aided in this respect by their position, Western New York is peopled principally by New Englanders, Ohio is connected with the interests of the West, and Maryland as a slave State, with those of the South. Whilst New England is the head, the Middle States, and especially New York and Pennsylvania (the Empire and the Keystone States), are the heart of the Union, the centre of all her interests.

Though the Middle States wield in fact the political power of the Union, yet nine out of the thirteen Presidents of the United States were Southerners, and the great majority of the government officials in Washington, and of the officers in the army, belong to the South.

3. The South, divided from the North and West by Mason's and Dixon's line, and by the Missouri compromise-boundary, includes fourteen States— Virginia, Kentucky, Tennessee, Missouri, Arkansas, Texas, Louisiana, Alabama, Georgia, Florida, the two Carolinas, Delaware, and in some respect Maryland. The link which unites so many States into one political body, the interest to which they subordinate all their jealousies, the "peculiar institution," which has developed their character, is SLAVERY. Missouri and Maryland, and even Kentucky and Virginia, are, we might say, only nominally slave States; they are peopled by agriculturists not by planters, and the abolition of slavery would, by no means, disturb all their interests, nor ruin the landed proprietors; but, though their prosperity is unconnected with slavery, those States are as jealous in watching their State rights, and as obstinately cling to their "peculiar institution," as South Carolina or Mississippi, because their pride refuses to yield to the threats of the northern abolitionists. Since the first establishment of the colonies, long before a slave was introduced into them, the character of the South has always been entirely different from that of New England. Younger sons of English families, adventurous cavaliers, settled in "the mother of States and Statesmen," Virginia, and in the

Carolinas; French adventurers of the same kind occupied the banks of the Mississippi, and an aristocratical stamp still characterises their descendants. Though the South remains behind New England in general instruction, and behind the Middle States in wealth and enterprise, yet the Southerners rule over their sharp northern neighbours in council and office. The departments at Washington are filled with them. Work is, in the South, as in Europe, not honourable in itself; none but the lawyer, the great merchant, and the physician, are acknowledged by the planters as gentlemen, and as their equals. There is no social equality between them and the shopkeepers and mechanics; and manual labour degrades the white in society. Slaves till the ground for the planter, who generally has no professional occupation, and has therefore leisure for the study of politics, and for political intrigues. From his youth accustomed to command, his individual impulses are more strongly developed than in the North. He lives in a grand style, and in his hospitality resembles the aristocrat of north-eastern Europe; susceptible and hot-headed, he is inclined to maintain his opinions by his fist, and always ready to demand, and to give satisfaction, with his brace of pistols or his rifle. The South is the country of large estates, of elegant houses, of carriages and four, of sports and races; but, also, of heavy mortgages, of pistols and bowie knives, of duels and affrays, and hereditary feuds. The lower classes are degraded; they shun

labour, because labour is the attribute of slavery;
they are illiterate, because the white population is
not dense enough to establish and to maintain
free schools, the newspapers are less numerous,
because they find no readers, and, as a general
result, the railways, canals, and steamers are scarce.
The Potomac teems not with sails and chimneys,
and the large floating palaces at the Lévée of "the
Crescent city," are all owned by Westerners. Every
shoe, every coat, every handle of an axe in the plantations are manufactured in New England, New York,
or Ohio. But Georgia forms an exception in this
respect, it is a manufacturing State, covered with a
net of railroads, growing in wealth and industry, and is
called therefore the Massachusetts of the South. She
was settled originally as a free State, and considerable infusion of New England blood has imparted to
her the spirit of industrial enterprise. But in general,
we can say that the South grows cotton, tobacco, and
rice, that it breeds horses and slaves, and furnishes
statesmen to the Union.

4. As Maryland forms the transition from the
Middle States to the South, so do Kentucky and
Missouri from the South to the West; to the West
belongs, besides these two, the States of Indiana,
Illinois, Michigan, Wisconsin, and Iowa, and, in
some measure, Ohio. It is a young agricultural
country, the home of the Sunday-schools, the terres-
trial paradise of the oppressed German and Irish
peasant, the land of independent small farmers; it is

the most democratic and equal society on earth. Frankness, disinterestedness, and hospitality characterise the Westerner. Unrefined in his manners, and sometimes rough, and even repulsive in his appearance, he is always ready to assist his neighbour, who has settled on the adjoining field, whom he never has seen before, and whose language perhaps he does not understand. He helps him in building the loghouse, he lends him his plough, and seeks with him the stray sheep, or the stolen horse, over the prairie.

The English had in their colonies always favoured large estates, and discountenanced or forbade squatting and small settlements, in order to raise artificially a population of daily labourers, who were to cultivate for wages the fields of the larger proprietors; and even the earliest law framed by Congress for the sale of the public lands, provided for its disposal to purchasers in tracts of 4000 acres each, and did not allow the selling of a smaller quantity. But, as early as 1800, an act of Congress broke up all such restrictions. Government land is sold in the new States, not only by the section of 640 acres, but also by the half and quarter section; and in the West we find scarcely a settlement larger than a section, whilst the quarter section is the average. A hundred and sixty acres are not too large to be cultivated by the hands of the farmer himself and of his numerous family, but are large enough, not only to maintain the family but also to afford the means of giving instruction to the children. Labour for wages is scarcer here because it is so easy to become an independent agriculturist. The settler is not unaware of the benefits of instruction, but his country, however, is yet too young and its resources not developed enough for a system of free daily schools; the Sunday-school is, therefore, the place where he as well as his children resort to, for general instruction. In the same way as the free schools form the most important and principal occupation of the Secretary of State in the New England States and New York, and are often visited by the Governor, the Sunday-schools are an object of peculiar importance for the administration of the western States, where you often may meet the Governor teaching the children and grown-up persons who fill the rooms. The West has, by this means, become an agricultural republic, with far-spreading elementary instruction, peopled by the hardiest, boldest, and most enduring nation of the world, to whom the unceasing contact and struggle with savage nature has imparted that bodily health and strength, and that mental vigour and soundness, which characterise the Kentucky hunter of old, and the modern pioneer of Iowa, Wisconsin, and Minnesota. Yet farther west, are the half-savage trappers of the forest, the theocratical Mormons of the Salt Lake, the reckless, adventurous miners of California, and the settlers and squatters of Oregon, all destined to form nations different from the East, and the South, and the West, but not yet numerous and developed enough to be described as such.

IV. AMERICAN PARTIES AND THEIR PRINCIPLES.

Not only the constitution and political configuration
of America is entirely different from the constitutions
of Europe ; the political parties too, stand on a different basis. Wherever political parties are allowed
to exist in the old world, they belong naturally to
two great groups, the conservative and progressive,
with their further shades of retrogression and radical-
ism. In the United States, on the contrary, there
are Progressists and Retrogrades, and Conservatives
amongst the Whigs, as well as amongst the Democrats;
and if we inquire about their principles, we shall
find the parties divided within themselves in respect
of nearly all the political questions before Congress.
The silver-grey Whigs are allied to the old Hunker
Democrats, and the Seward-men are often voting with
barn-burners and locofocos. The last *platforms* (thus
they call in America the programmes)—of the two
great parties, the Democrats, and democratic Whigs,
are nearly identical, and yet the party-strife is going
on as intensely as ever. Superficial observers are
therefore readily induced to say that it must be a
personal struggle, and a politieal war of two clans for
offices and spoils,—for the 25,000 dollars a year of
the President, and the sixty millions of patronage,
which, according to the custom and eternal laws of
war, belong to the victor, and are to be divided
amongst the party. But when we investigate not
only their platforms, but also the tendencies of
parties, we shall find that there is a real and most

substantial difference between them, much more important than at first it seems, and that the democrats and democratic Whigs, not only differ from one another on questions of political economy, but are really representatives of political principles so different, that even the questions of conservatism and progress are subordinate to them, though the resemblance of their platforms, their agreement about the questions which are at this moment the most prominent, and the splitting of both parties in respect of other great questions, hide their real difference.

As to the history of the parties in America, it is sufficient to mention here, that originally there prevailed the same denominations in the colonies as in the mother country, and that the Tories sided during the war with the English. Many of them left the States with the English, others who had made themselves prominent, were expelled, the remainder were necessarily converted into good Whigs; Toryism ceased with the war of independence. But the Whigs were soon themselves divided into Republicans, who maintained the absolute sovereignity of each of the thirteen States, and saw a danger for liberty in every attempt at union, and Federalists, who had no great confidence in the successful establishment of popular free institutions based on democracy and universal suffrage, who therefore wished to dam the flood of democracy by strengthening and giving more permanence to the executive and to the Senate. They did not like frequent popular elections, and a direct influence of the people on the legislation; they feared that America should pass through anarchy to despotism, and were therefore not altogether averse to a monarchical form of government. Their views remained in minority, and as the constitution,—such as it was established in 1788, by a compromise of the opposite principles,— seemed to them at least superior to the loose confederation, as it had existed since the establishment of independence, the principal men of the party exerted their talents in its support; but they always favoured restrictive measures, and a narrow policy. Being a kind of intellectual aristocrats, liberal Conservatives, like Monsieur Guizot,—they had no faith in the people, and shunned the contact with the masses.

But the Anti-federalists soon carried the day; Jefferson laid down the broad principles of Democracy, recognised the right of every man to freedom and equality, maintained the rights of the Indians to the occupation of their lands, removed every obstacle to immigration, and, by the purchase qf Louisiana and of the country west of the Mississippi, he gave to the United States their natural frontier, and the possibility of expansion. He is the father of American Democracy, though not of the present democratic party, which acknowledges only a part of Jefferson's principles as its own. The democratic party, as it stands now, is less Jeffersonian than Jacksonian, and has developed itself and gained strength principally by the contest about the United States Bank and the disposal of the surplus in the United States treasury; by the measure of the annexation of Texas, and the war with Mexico. Though all those questions have been long ago disposed of, they yet occupy a considerable place in the official declaration of the principles of the party; they are the trophies of the Democrats, who think it expedient to recall their successful political struggles to the mind of the masses. The last democratic platform is really rather a review of the past than a programme of the future; they evidently do not like to commit themselves on the important questions which are to be decided under the next presidency, as the homestead bill, the improvement of the lakes and of the Mississippi, the foreign policy, and the tariff. The Whigs expressed themselves upon three of those questions more especially, but they speak as little about their principles as their opponents; both agree in regard to the slave question, and both, of course, promise an economical government; they express their confidence in the patriotism and intelligence of the American people; they both acknowledge that the federal government is of a limited character, and recognise the rights of the individual States.

Comparing, therefore, the two platforms, we do not become wiser as to the questions which divide the parties. One of them is for liberty and order, the other for order and liberty. One is liberal conservative, the other is conservative liberal. We see only that both are for the presidency on behalf of their nominees, and for the government patronage for the party and party leaders.

In order to substantiate these assertions, we subjoin the two party programmes, as they were laid down by the party conventions at Baltimore, in June, 1852 :—

" Resolutions of the Democratic National Convention.

Resolved,—That the American Democracy place their trust in the intelligence, the patriotism, and the discriminating justice of the American people.

Resolved,—That we regard this as a distinctive feature of our political creed, which we are proud to maintain before the world, as the great moral element in a form of government springing from and upheld by the popular will; and we contrast it with the creed and practice of Federalism under whatever name or form, which seeks to palsy the will of the constituent, and which conceives no imposture too monstrous for the popular credulity.

Resolved, therefore, that, entertaining these views, the Democratic party of this Union, through their delegates assembled in a General Convention of the States, coming together in a spirit of concord, of devotion to the doctrines and faith of a free representative government, and appealing to their fellow-citizens for the rectitude of their intentions, renew and reassert, before the American people, the declarations of principles avowed by them, when, on former occasions, in General Convention, they presented their candidates for the popular suffrages.

1. That the Federal Government is one of limited powers, derived solely from the Constitution, and the grants of power made therein ought to be strictly construed by all the departments and agents of the

" Platform of the Whig Party.

The Whigs of the United States, in convention assembled, adhering to the great conservative republican principles by which they are controlled and governed, and now as ever relying upon the intelligence of the American people, with an abiding confidence in their capacity for self-government, and their continued devotion to the constitution and the Union, do proclaim the following as the political sentiments and determination, for the establishment and maintenance of which their national organization, as a party, is effected :—

The government of the United States is of a limited character, and it is confined to the exercise of powers expressly granted by the Constitution, and such as may be necessary and proper for carrying the granted powers into full execution, and that all powers not thus granted or necessarily implied, are expressly reserved to the States respectively, and to the people.

The State Governments should be held secure in their reserved rights, and the general Government sustained in its constitutional powers, and the Union should be revered and watched over as " the palladium of our liberties.

Government; and that it is inexpedient and dangerous to exercise doubtful constitutional powers.

2. That the Constitution does not confer upon the General Government the power to commence and carry on a *general* system of Internal Improvements.

3. That the Constitution does not confer authority upon the Federal Government, directly or indirectly, to assume the debts of the several States, contracted for local Internal Improvements, or other State purposes; nor would such assumption be just or expedient.

4. That justice and sound policy forbid the Federal Government to foster one branch of industry to the detriment of any other, or to cherish the interests of one portion to the injury of another portion of our common country; that every citizen, and every section of the country, has a right to demand and insist upon an equality of rights and privileges, and to complete and ample protection of persons and property from domestic violence or foreign aggression.

5. That it is the duty of every branch of the Government to enforce and practise the most rigid economy in conducting our public affairs, and that no more revenue ought to be raised than is required to defray the necessary expenses of the Government, and for the gradual but certain extinction of the public debt.

6. That Congress has no power to charter a national bank; that we believe such an institution one of deadly hostility to the best interests of the country,

The constitution vests in Congress the power to open and repair harbours, and remove obstructions from navigable rivers. It is expedient that Congress should exercise such power, whenever such improvements are necessary for the common defence, and for the protection and facility of commerce with foreign nations, or among the States—said improvements being in every instance national and general in their character.

[No corresponding Whig resolution.]

Revenue sufficient for the expenses of an economical administration of government, in time of peace, ought to be derived from a duty on imposts and not from direct taxes, and in laying such duties, sound policy requires a just discrimination, whereby suitable encouragement may be afforded to American industry, equally to all classes, and to all portions of the country.

[No corresponding Whig resolution.]

dangerous to our republican institutions and the liberties of the people, and calculated to place the business of the country within the control of a concentrated money power, and above the laws and the will of the people; and that the results of democratic legislation, in this and all other financial measures upon which issues have been made between the two political parties of the country, have demonstrated to candid and practical men of all parties their soundness, safety, and utility, in all business pursuits.

7. That the separation of the moneys of the Government from banking institutions is indispensable for the safety of the funds of the Government and the rights of the people.

8. That the liberal principles embodied by Jefferson in the Declaration of Independence, and sanctioned in the Constitution, which makes ours the land of liberty, and the asylum of the oppressed of every nation, have ever been cardinal principles in the Democratic faith; and every attempt to abridge the privilege of becoming citizens and the owners of soil among us, ought to be resisted with the same spirit which swept the Alien and Sedition laws from our statute book.

9. That Congress has no power under the Constitution to interfere with or control the domestic institutions of the several States, and that such States are the sole and proper judges of everything appertaining to their own affairs, not prohibited by the Constitution; that all efforts of the Abolitionists or others,

[No corresponding Whig resolution.]

[No corresponding Whig resolution.]

The Federal and State governments are parts of one system, alike necessary for the common prosperity, peace and security, and ought to be regarded alike with a cordial, habitual, and immoveable attachment. Respect for the authority of each, and acquiescence in the just constitutional measures of made to induce Congress to interfere with questions of Slavery, or to take incipient steps in relation thereto, are calculated to lead to the most alarming and dangerous consequences; and that all such efforts have an inevitable tendency to diminish the happiness of the people, and endanger the stability and permanency of the Union, and ought not to be countenanced by any friend of our political institutions.

Resolved,—That the foregoing proposition covers, and was intended to embrace, the whole subject of Slavery agitation in Congress; and therefore · the Democratic party of the Union, standing on this national platform, will abide by, and adhere to, a faithful execution of the acts known as the Compromise measures settled by the last Congress—the act for reclaiming fugitives from service or labour included: which act, being designed to carry out an express provision of the Constitution, cannot with fidelity thereto be repealed, nor so changed as to destroy or impair its efficiency.

Resolved,—That the Democratic party will resist all attempts at renewing in Congress, or out of it, the agitation of the Slavery question, under whatever shape or colour the attempt may be made.

Resolved,—That the proceeds of the Public Lands ought to be sacredly applied to the national objects specified in the Constitution; and that we are opposed to any law for the distribution of such proceeds among the States, as alike inexpedient in policy, and repugnant to the Constitution.

each are duties required by the plainest considerations of national, of State, and of individual welfare.

That the series of resolutions known as the Compromise, including the Fugitive Slave law, are received and acquiesced in by the Whig party of the United States as a settlement in principle and substance—a final settlement—of the dangerous and exciting subjects which they embrace; and so far as the Fugitive Slave law is concerned, we will maintain the same, and insist on its strict enforcement, until time and experience shall demonstrate the necessity of further legislation against evasion or abuses, but not impairing its efficiency; and we deprecate all future agitation of the slavery question as dangerous to our peace, and we will discountenance all efforts at the renewal or continuance of such agitation in Congress, or out of it, whenever, wherever, or howsoever the attempt may be made, and will maintain this system of measures, as policy essential to the nationality of the Whig party, and the integrity of the Union.

Resolved,—That we are decidedly opposed to taking from the President the qualified veto power, by which he is enabled, under restrictions and responsibilities amply sufficient to guard the public interest, to suspend the passage of a bill whose merits cannot secure the approval of two-thirds of the Senate and House of Representatives until the judgment of the people can be obtained thereon, and which has saved the American people from the corrupt and tyrannical domination of the Bank of the United States, and from a corrupting system of general internal improvements.

Resolved,—That the Democratic party will faithfully abide by and uphold the principles laid down in the Kentucky and Virginia Resolutions of 1792 and 1798, and in the report of Mr. Madison, to the Virginia' Legislature in 1799; that it adopts those principles as constituting one of the main foundations of its political creed, and is resolved to carry them out in their obvious meaning and import.

Resolved,—That the war with Mexico, upon all the principles of patriotism and the laws of nations, was a just and necessary war on our part, in which no American citizen should have shown himself opposed to his country, and neither morally nor physically, by word or deed, given aid and comfort to the enemy.

Resolved,—That we rejoice at the restoration of friendly relations with our sister Republic of Mexico, and earnestly desire for her all the blessings and prosperity which we enjoy under republican insti-

[No corresponding Whig resolution.]

[No corresponding Whig resolution.]

[No corresponding Whig resolution.]

[No corresponding Whig resolution.]

tutions, and we congratulate the American people on the results of that war, which have so manifestly justified the policy and conduct of the Democratic party, and insured to the United States, indemnity for the past and security for the future.

Resolved,—That in view of the condition of popular institutions in the old world, a high and sacred duty is devolved with increased responsibility upon the Democracy of this country, as the party of the people, to uphold and maintain the rights of every State, and thereby the Union of the States, and to sustain and advance among them constitutional liberty, by continuing to resist all monopolies and exclusive legislation for the benefit of the few at the expense of the many, and by a vigilant and constant adherence to these principles and compromises of the Constitution, which are broad enough and strong enough to embrace and uphold the Union as it is, and the Union as it should be, in the full expansion of the energies and capacity of this great and progressive people."

That while struggling freedom every where enlists the warmest sympathy of the Whig party, we still adhere to the doctrines of the father of his country, as announced in his farewell address, of keeping ourselves free from all entangling alliances with foreign countries, and of never quitting our own to stand upon foreign ground—that our mission as a Republic is not to propagate our opinions, or impose on other countries our form of government, by artifice or force, but to teach by example, and show by our success, moderation, and justice, the blessings of self-government, and the advantages of free institutions.

That, where the people make and control the Government, they should obey its constitution, laws and treaties, as they should retain their self-respect, and the respect which they claim and will enforce from foreign powers."

Notwithstanding this similarity of the two platforms no fusion of the two parties is possible, each of
them is held together by unwritten principles, understood by every American, though not published in
the platform.

The object to which the Whigs aspire, for the
individual States as well as for the Union, is *an
aristocracy* in the literal sense of the word—the
government of the best, with the aim of taking the
lead of the people; a government, therefore, which
has the intention and the means to do good.   Their
principal aim is to enrich the nation, to make her
industry independent of Europe, to develop the
resources of the country—not to extend its territory.
As a rule, they do not court the masses, but they
endeavour to raise the standard of their morals and
of their education.   They do not object to higher
taxation for the construction of canals and railways
by the individual States; they advocate the protection
of American steam navigation by premiums, of their
fisheries by bounties, of their manufactures by a
high tariff.   They demand that the States should
establish higher institutions for science; that Congress
should open and repair harbours, and remove the
obstructions of rivers; and are friendly to an expan-
sive banking system.   They are opposed to all war,
but ready to confide power to the heads of the States
or Federal administration: they would give to the
people the right of only electing representatives, not
of binding them by instructions.   To sum up their

principles in a few words, the Whigs represent authority, commerce, wealth, and centralising tendencies.

The Democrats, on the other side, take it for granted, that Government is nothing but a necessary evil. They think that, by the frailty of human nature, every Government is too apt to extend its power, to encroach upon the rights of the people, and to squander the public income. They require, therefore, a Government which does as little as possible; they claim only that it should not obstruct the free development of the people, according to its own wants and requirements. They like military glory, and territorial extension. Government, according to them, must be powerful and commanding towards the foreigner; protecting the citizens and their pursuits abroad, but not interfering in any way with their concerns at home—it has always to act according to the expressed wishes of the people, which has the right of directing the Government. The Democrats, therefore, are free-traders in principle, and advocates of a gold currency; they leave the construction of canals and railways to the speculation of individuals and of companies, and are generally averse to the Government support of such undertakings. They oppose the increase of the standing army, but war is always popular with them, because it extends the territory of the Union and rouses the slumbering energies of the masses, to whose will and to whose passions they readily submit. Their representatives and senators are strictly *delegates*, and have to give up their seat if their instructions do not agree with their convictions. They affirm, as a cardinal truth, that the world is governed too much. They are enemies of centralisation and of all restriction, and as every law is a restriction, they do not like much legislating, fully convinced that the people is always able to govern itself well, without being led by the officials. The Democrats represent liberty, self-government of the people, agriculture, and territorial expansion.

It is quite natural that both the parties often carry their principles too far: that Democrats sometimes flatter and excite the worst prejudices of the people, and become Demagogues, whilst Whigs sometimes seclude themselves from the masses, and endeavour to transplant the aristocratical distinctions of European society into the New World. Democracy, triumphant in New Hampshire, opposed the construction of railways for a long time, and the Louisiana Convention refused to the Government the power of renewing the Bank-charters. On the other side, Pennsylvania involved herself under the Whigs, in a debt of 44,000,000 dollars for railways and canals, extending them in many unprofitable directions, without completing the net; and the bursting of the bank bubble in many States was the result of too much latitude given by the Whigs to the banking system. But such exaggerations never last long, and lead, after a party defeat, to a fair settlement of the question.

The Whigs have now no intention of chartering a
'United States' Bank, or of abandoning an efficient
public control over the issue of bank notes; they have
established a sound banking system in different States;
and the Democratic States, with the exception perhaps of Arkansas, Texas, and California, collect their
revenues in bank notes, deposit them in banks, and
are at all times borrowing from banks, or trusting
them in a hundred ways, in spite of the platform.
The growing importance of the Mississippi valley
has forced upon the Democrats the necessity of
advocating likewise the improvement of the Western
waters by the federal Government, and the larger
grants of public land, for canals and railway purposes
in the West, have not been opposed by them in the
session of 1852. In the same way it is probable, that
as Pennsylvania, Missouri, Illinois, Wisconsin, and
Michigan, claim protection for their iron and lead
industry, the import duties on iron and lead will not
be objected to by the Democrats. Colonel Benton,
at least, one of the great democratic leaders, declared
himself lately against the *ad valorem*, and for the
specific duty in general, and especially pledged himself for the support of protection for iron industry.
As to the Mexican war, whatever may be the opinion
of the Whigs about its injustice, I never heard that
there would be amongst them one single man, who
would now consent to give up either California or
New Mexico. Yet the questions of protection, of
general improvements, of the United States' Bank,

and the Mexican war, remain the topics for all the
political speeches in the respective party-meetings.

It is natural, from the above mentioned facts, that
the great bulk of the manufacturers, bankers, merchants, and of the wealthier inhabitants of the great
cities, are Whigs; the commercial interest is theirs,
whilst democracy sways over all the agricultural and
planting States and communities, and especially over
the slaveholding South; as non-interference on the
part of the federal government,—which, according to
the Democrats, must follow the wishes of the people,—
gives more guarantee of stability to their peculiar
institution than a strong and meddling Whig administration going a-head of public opinion. The
Irish and German emigrants are also a continuous
source of accession of power to the Democratic party,
as its very name is a bait for the multitude coming
from Europe, though European Democracy is somewhat different from the American Democratic party.
The Whigs feel this very strongly, and they have
therefore appended the designation of *Democratic* to
their party-name. As far as I was able to find, this
measure has remained without success, and the Irish
and Germans take the Whigs generally for enemies,
not only of the Democratic party, but also of Democratic institutions. They do it so much the more, as a
set of narrow-minded Conservative Whigs, in the sea-
port cities, have constituted themselves as the *Native
Party*, wishing to restrict the laws of naturalisation,
thus to withhold the right of voting in elections from

all the emigrants, and reserving the vote for those who were born in America. Some years ago the native party found many theoretical supporters amongst the Whigs, and some few even amongst the Democrats; but after having created ill feeling amongst the emigrants, and driven all the naturalised citizens to the democratic ranks, it went on declining, and is only in few places still of some local importance.

But the party-division does not stop here. In the ranks of the Democrats, as well as of the Whigs, there are different shades, each of them characterised by a nickname, and all quarrelling with one another, though at the elections fighting under the common banner against the opposite party. The Conservative Democrats, who sturdily oppose every progressive measure, got the nickname of *Old Hunkers*. They are always at hand when spoils are to be divided, and often got a share even of the Whig Government contracts. The progressive wing of Democracy, was originally called *Locofocos,* or concisely *Locos,* from the fact, that at a great democratic meeting, where the Old Hunkers, after having carried their resolutions in a hurried way, adjourned and put the lights out, the progressive section remained in the dark hall, and lighting the gas up by a locofoco-match (the American name for lucifer-matches) continued the meeting, and reconsidered the resolutions of the Conservatives. The name of Locofoco, however, is now applied to the whole party : for, to the Whigs every Democrat

is a firebrand. The thorough-going liberal Democrats, got therefore, in New York, another name,
viz., *Barnburners,* from a phrase of one of their
orators, who said that they must burn the barns in
order to expel the rats; in Maine they are called
Wildcats. The *Softshells* form the transition between
the Hunkers and Barnburners,—they are half-and-
halfs, whilst the *Hardshell Hunkers* are the most
Conservative party in the world, averse to every social
and intellectual movement. During our stay in the
United States, a new party distinction arose amongst
the Democrats, *Young America* comprising all the
ardent and generous minds of the party, in opposition
to the *Old Fogies,* as the professional politicians were
called by them.

The Conservative-Whigs, the Fillmore men, are
termed *Silvergreys,* as one of their chiefs,—when
attacked for his clinging to the old statesmen, who
had devised the Fugitive Slave Bill as a compromise
between the South and the North,—exclaimed, that
he remained rather a private amongst the *Silvergreys,*
than a leader amongst the *Woolly-heads.* Those
Woolly-heads, or *Seward-men,* are the Liberals
amongst the Whigs, and got their origin in the
political struggle about the compromise. They are
opposed to the territorial extension of slavery; they
wish to remove slavery from the pale of general legislation, therefore they endeavour to have it abolished
in the district of Columbia and the territories, and
they made a strong opposition against the Fugitive

Slave-law, because it did not secure a trial by jury to the defendant. They agree in respect to this question entirely with the *Freesoilers*, who belonged originally to the Democrats, but had seceded from them in 1848, whilst the Seward party remained in communion with the Whigs, in spite of the platform of 1852. Instead of forming a separate organisation, they endeavour to carry their theories by getting first a majority for them in the party itself. This example was followed lately by many of the democratic bolters of 1848, amongst whom we notice the originators of the name and party, Martin and John Van Buren. But some of the original Freesoilers remained beyond the pale of the Whigs and Democrats, and were reinforced by many noble-hearted men, principally in Massachusetts, New York, and Ohio, who do not care for momentary success. They called themselves at first the *Liberty-party*, and got in Massachusetts the balance of power in their hands; but knowing the force of names, they constituted themselves, at the late convention at Pittsburgh, as *Free Democracy*. Their creed is given in the resolution of the Boston Ratification Meeting :—

" Resolved,—That no man on this earth can own another man: that the slave power in this country must be destroyed; that the Fugitive Slave Law should be repealed; that human bondage in *the territories and in the district* (Columbia), should be abolished; that all the new States should be free States; that our Government should acknowledge the independence of Hayti;

that the rights of American coloured citizens in every
State ought to be protected; that the general Government is a great organisation of freedom, and should
go for it every where; that it should always be on the
side of the weak against the strong, the slave against
the tyrant, the people against the despot."

The *Abolitionists* proper, the "Garrison-men,"
are a less numerous, but energetic party; they
denounce slavery in the scriptural language of the
prophets, which is not entirely Parliamentary.

The parties in America are organised in a different
way than in Europe. I already have mentioned that
Conservatives and Progressists form but different
wings in the same party, held together by the *Electoral
Ticket*. It is not the difference of opinions, which
marks a new party, but a separate nomination
of candidates for the State and Federal offices. The
Seward-men, the Van Buren Freesoilers, the Free
Democrats, and the Abolitionists are but different
shades of the same colour. Yet the Seward-men
remain within the pale of Whiggism, the Democrat
Freesoilers do not bolt from the great democratic
party, but the Free Democrats have put up a different
ticket, and the Abolitionists proper, quarrelling with
them about terms, secede even from them, and withhold their votes from the federal elections, preferring
to be the theoretical *Apostles* of their principles, than
Statesmen with practical influence on the affairs of
the country. They preach principles and opinions,
and do not care in what way they are to be carried

without endangering the Union, and without convulsing the South;—Prophets of evil, without advising
the means how to avoid it. The Seward-men are
aware of it, that a repeal or even a modification of
the Fugitive Slave Law, is for the present impossible;
they therefore confine themselves to the measure of
abolishing slavery in the district of Columbia. The
Free Democrats intend besides, the repeal of the
Fugitive Slave Law, in order that the question of
slavery should be excluded from the federal legislation,
and the decision of it should remain entirely with
the Southern States. The Abolitionists preach that
slavery is immoral, a sin against the *Law of God*, the
higher law, and therefore cannot be the object of any
legislation. This is the difference between them.*
But the direct influence of the Abolitionists is very
limited, on account of their violence, which gives to
the Southern slaveholders a pretext for declamations
not less violent, against the encroachments of the
North on the rights of the South.

The *Secessionists* of the South, are the very reverse
of the Abolitionists of the North; like them, they are
not caring for the general interests of the United States,
and the natural and political links between them;
they consider every measure exclusively from the point
of view of slavery, they boldly express that they

* For the English reader we must observe, that the authoress of
Uncle Tom's Cabin,' Mrs. H. B. Stowe, Mr. Cassius M. Clay, Horace
Greeley, the Senators Chase, Hale, Sumner, and Seward, all disclaim
the Abolitionist designation; they do not approve of Mr. Garrison's
violence and the unparliamentary proceedings of his party.

cling more to their "peculiar institution" than to
the federal constitution, and pretend that the right
of secession from the Union belongs to every individual State, and that such a secession cannot be
taken for treason. They had considerable influence
in the South during the discussions of the Fugitive
Slave Law, principally in their original seat South
Carolina, but I never could ascertain whether they
were in earnest with their threats or not. So much
is sure, that they carried their point, and their success
may encourage them again, to renew a manœuvre
which frightens the North, gives rise to many fine
speeches on the danger and importance of the Union,
and affords periodically the precious occasion for the
leading statesmen to save the Union and the country.
Their opponents in the South were the *Union-men,
Union Whigs,* as well as *Union Democrats,* who deem
the difficulties about slavery settled for ever by the
Compromise and Fugitive Slave Law, whilst the Secessionists, or, as they now call themselves, *Southern
Rights Men,* are not satisfied with this measure, but
think it insufficient to protect the peculiar institution.

A new division of the party interests is "looming
in the future"—the combination of the Western
agricultural inland States against the sea-coast States.
The Westerners think their interests slighted by the
land system, and complain that the sea-coast States
are jealous of a new and rival seaboard on the Pacific;
the "new thirteen" would halve and distribute their
importance and natural monopoly of all foreign com-

merce. But the decennial census of 1850 gives in the ensuing Congress, a majority to the people residing beyond the Alleghanies, in the great basin of the Continent, and one of its first proceedings will surely be to pass the Homestead-bill (which will change the system of the public land), to establish measures for the improvement of the Western waters, and perhaps the great railway to California, which will satisfy the West.

Since the sovereign self-government of the States, and the frequent elections give a chance of a fair trial to every theory, the parties often avail themselves of the theoretical questions of the day, which then become the issues of the party contests and triumphs. Several years back Freemasonry became a party question, and was fiercely attacked by the Whigs, who denounced all secret societies. But this agitation has entirely subsided, as the Americans generally are overfond of secret societies, and lodges of Masons and of Odd Fellows are to be found all over the Union, among Whigs and Democrats, through all classes of society.

The Temperance question became of late also of political importance. Taken up by the Whigs in New England, who, in order to check the hard drinking propensities of the people, endeavoured to enforce teatotalism by legislation, forbidding altogether the sale of spirits, except on the prescription of the physician.* The temperance question got an additional

---

* An old adage gives the lesson to the people of Boston :
    "Men of Boston! don't make long orations;
    Men of Boston! don't take strong potations."

power by the establishment of the order of the *Sons of Temperance,* which was organised under masonic forms ; and the Liquor Law, as it was called, closing all the rum-shops and gin-palaces, and forbidding the sale of all spirits whatsoever, has been carried in Maine, Massachusetts, Rhode Island, and Minnesota. Whether this remarkable restriction on personal liberty, sanctioned in Maine by the overwhelming majority of the population, will be long endured by the masses, I cannot predict; but in the meantime the temperance and rum-selling party, both recruited promiscously from the ranks of Whigs and Democrats, became of considerable importance in the local and State elections.

Another semisecret society, which was formed during our stay in the United States, and whose bearing upon party politics may become of consequence, is *the Order of the Lone Star,* started principally by the Southern Democrats, with the avowed aim of revolutionising Cuba, and annexing " the jewel of the Antilles" to the United States. Those who countenance such enterprises are called Filibusteros by the Northern Whigs, and denounced as pirates ; but the success of Texas is a too attractive precedent for the enterprising and adventurous youth of the South, whom the melancholy fate of General Lopez and his companions do not deter. "We failed," said one of the invaders of Cuba to me—a gentleman who had just returned from his African prison at Ceuta, " therefore we are pirates, had we succeeded, Lopez would have been a second William the Conqueror."

The Antirenters of New York are a lawless combination of the lessees of the large Van Ransellaer property, who declare that feudal tenure is against the spirit of American liberty, and therefore are not only unwilling to pay the rents, but set at defiance the law, forcibly resist the execution of the sentence passed against them, and commit agrarian outrages on those who pay their rents, or support the enforcement of the law. This conspiracy has however, in a certain degree, carried its object; the proprietors were compelled for a money consideration to waive their claims to rent and ownership; and the majority of the farmers have already become proprietors. But there are in the State of New York, besides the practical Antirenters, also theoretical *Antirenters,* who are anxious to abolish the Van Ransellaer title by law, and who excuse the agrarian outrages committed in connexion with this property. For a party they are not numerous enough.

Such are the general outlines of the political configuration of North America, and of the principles and subdivisions of the parties, modifying the national character in the different parts of the Union so far, that it is really difficult to pronounce a judgment, either on the political feelings, or even on the social manners and customs of the people. Notwithstanding the community of language and government, there are as great national differences in America as

in Europe. As to the state of parties, the foreigner
who measures them by the rule of European politics
of conservatism and progress, is *entirely* bewildered.
The European measure is not applicable to trans-
Atlantic relations.

CHAPTER IV.

PHILADELPHIA—BALTIMORE.

1. PHILADELPHIA—THE RECEPTION—MRS. MOTT—THE
PRISON—INDEPENDENCE HALL.

(*From Mrs. Pulszky's Diary.*)

Dec. 24th.—Several gentlemen of the committee of arrangement for the welcome of Kossuth in Philadelphia arrived in New York, to convey us to the " Quaker City." They decided that we ladies should precede the gentlemen, and instead of repairing direct to Philadelphia, should go first to a country-house on the Susquehanna.

We started on the morning of the 22d of December. The weather was not precisely favourable; and though we went by rail, and the car was provided with a stove, we suffered much from cold, draught, and wet; for as the people expected Kossuth to come along with us, at every station they poured in, and turned the carriage into a thoroughfare. We proceeded very slowly; the masses of snow had so rapidly accumulated, that it could not be shoveled off in time. The windows of our carriage were soon totally frozen, so that we could not see anything of the scenery around, and were limited for information and amusement to the conversation of the gentlemen who accompanied us. Mr. F * * * was very kind and obliging, readily answering all my questions about the farms along the road, at which I tried very hard to peep, rubbing the pane with my handkerchief. Here and there I perceived plain houses, with but few barns and stables; farming seemed to be carried on on a small scale, apparently by the proprietor himself, with but few hands to help him.

Mr. * * *, one of the gentlemen who accompanied us, was a native of Germany. He had, as he told me himself, made his fortune in America, whither he had come as a boy; but his principles he certainly had not moulded on the Republican institutions of his adopted country. He highly approved of the *coup d'état* of Louis Napoleon, advocating the wisdom of the measure, which, according to him, was sure to succeed lastingly, because Europe was not fit for freedom, and Russia was the only real power, and at last must rule over the whole world. Of Philadelphia he thought his own house the most interesting part, which he described with the relish of a *parvenu*, enumerating his splendid furniture, the sums it had cost him, and how well he could afford such luxury.

From the terminus a few minutes' ride took us to a slightly-built wooden house, obviously uninhabited for several months; there was all around the comfortless chill of unpeopled rooms. The master of the house had come up from Philadelphia to greet us, a most amiable and kind gentleman, who did his best for our accommodation; but neither hospitable cordiality, nor even a crackling fire in the chimney, can war.a the damp walls of a lonely summer-abode in December. A gentleman whom I had observed in the train, but with whom we were not acquainted, partook of our supper. Our host asked me who the person was, as he thought he had come with us. Finding that I could give no information, he inquired from the gentlemen of the Committee, but no one could tell; the stranger had introduced himself as belonging to our party, but without giving his name. After close investigation, the unexpected guest turned out to be a correspondent of the ' Courier and Enquirer,' the New York paper which ever railed at the cause of Hungary and all those connected with it.

On the morrow I beheld the Susquehanna river, which bends its course through the dale; an open ground separated our window from the borders of the stream. It was a smiling, cultivated landscape. Beyond the waters were young copses, but my eye sought in vain the forests of which we are reminded by the name of the State. Here nothing appeared primitive, nothing ancient, everything young and unfinished; no garden laid out round the cottage, no poultry-yard, nothing but board partitions hastily put up, to afford a temporary shelter to a carriage and horses; and the abode itself was, in fact, nothing but a nice edition of a log-house,—everything for utility, nothing for delight.

Towards evening we left for Philadelphia; the darkness, but faintly relieved by the plains of snow spreading on all sides, prevented us from distinguish-

ing any object. About eleven we reached the city.
The streets were as silent as the tall houses clustering
all round ; no vestige of the busy hum of a great town,
it seemed all hushed into rest. Even the United States
Hotel, where we slept, was perfectly quiet, and the
gaslight shone only in the parlours prepared for us.
The gentlemen of the Committee invited us to supper,
of which oysters formed the chief elements :* oyster-
soup, oyster-pie, fried oysters, and especially a cala-
bash of terapines—a ragout of delicately small turtles
—were relished by our hosts, who attempted to discuss
the probable results of the *coup d'état* of Napoleon,
but obviously knew little about European affairs.

Kossuth entered the city in the night, being
anxious to avoid costly demonstrations, that the
sympathy of the masses for the cause of Hungary
might not be wasted in pageantry. The municipality
of the city, however, did not think it politic to de-
prive the multitude of a show, and themselves of the
credit of a well-managed procession. Therefore, on
the morrow flags waved in the streets, the militia
and the members of different associations assembled
in various parts of the city, bands of music played in
the streets, and the people left the wharves, and the
shops, and their trades, to witness the festive "turn-
out," of which they themselves formed the main bulk
and the most interesting part.

Stately display enough there was, and this, I fear,

* William Penn mentions, in one of his letters to the Free Society
of Traders, "The oysters of Pennsylvania, six inches long."

drew the chief attention of too many a spectator who looked down comfortably from the windows. But the dense crowd in the streets, swelling like an avalanche, hurry past all the gaiety and grandeur, and rush to get a glimpse of that calm, melancholy countenance of the man who has struggled so firmly, and has not been crushed by defeat. They do not care for the approaching snow-storm, which fills the air with icy dampness; it is a great day for them, to welcome the Washington of a nation which is brave as they are themselves, though less fortunate.

It was a great demonstration; but poor Kossuth did not relish to be gazed at by an admiring people; he was worn out by his exertions in New York, where, during the last week, besides receiving innumerable deputations, he had made in a foreign language six great speeches,—a fact unprecedented in the annals of eloquence, especially in a time when the greatest orator of England is allowed by the public to commit plagiarisms, and to rehearse the same speech on two successive occasions. With Kossuth the task of the orator has remained pure from theatrical inanity. Eloquence with him is only the means of carrying conviction to the soul, not of dazzling the public by a series of elaborate phrases.

After the ceremony was over I mounted a sledge, and drove over the parts of the city most resorted to, and I found that the Quaker city has not lost the character of its origin. Solid neatness and thrifty simplicity prevail in the style of its houses and in

the dress of the pedestrians we met. Beneficent
institutions, prisons, almshouses, orphan asylums,
houses of refuge, were pointed out to me on every
step. The city does not strike as beautiful or attractive; no public monument stands here to please the
eye; yet there is the stamp of wealth and of commerce wherever we cast our glance on the buildings
and on the inhabitants, and we cannot help feeling
that the pulsation of life must be strong and genial
in these precincts, though it may in general be un-
adorned by the charms of art and somewhat monotonous. Every one I chanced to see in the streets
seemed to pursue a definite aim; they looked all so
serious and steady, even the rosy countenances of the
young girls. None of them stopt at a shop to review
the wares put up in its windows, and the very articles
displayed there show that this is a rich market for
useful objects, but rather a scanty one for elegant
superfluities. And if ever such were in demand here,
they certainly would be exhibited to-day, on Christmas Eve, when every child in the Christian world
expects some joyful present.

Dec. 25*th.*—I called on Mrs. Mott, the eminent
Quaker lady, to whom a mutual friend had given me
a letter. I have seldom seen a face more artistically
beautiful than that of Mrs. Lucretia Mott. She
looks like an antique cameo. Her features are so
markedly characteristic, that, if they were less noble,
they might be called sharp. Beholding her I felt

that great ideas and noble purposes must have grown
up with her mind, which have a singular power of
expression in her very movements. Her language is,
like her appearance, peculiar and transparent, and it
is only when she touches upon the slavery question
that her eye flashes with an indignation and her lips
quiver with a hasty impatience, disturbing the placid
harmony of her countenance and her conversation.
But though she so positively pronounces the views at
which she has arrived by self-made inquiry, yet she
mildly listens to every objection, and tries to con-
vince by the power of her arguments, untinged by
the slightest fanaticism. She expressed her warm
sympathy with the cause of Hungary, and her admiration of the genius of Kossuth; yet she blamed his
neutrality in the slavery question. I objected, that
as Kossuth claimed non-intervention as the sacred
law of nations, he was not called to interfere in a
domestic question of the United States, so intimately
connected with their constitution. But how can
Kossuth, the champion of liberty,—answered she—
not raise his voice in favour of the oppressed race?
to argue is surely not the same thing as to interfere.
I replied, that a question involving intricate domestic
interests, and for that very reason passions so bitter,
that even an allusion to it rouses sensitive jealousies,
certainly cannot be discussed by a foreigner with the
slightest chance of doing good; that the difficulty
of emancipation lies perhaps less in the lack of acknowledgment of the evils of slavery, than in the

hardness to advise the many of carrying emancipation without convulsing the financial interests of the slaveholders, and to do it in a constitutional way. For after all, this must be attended to, if the welfare of the whole community is not to be endangered, therefore this problem can only be solved practically by native American statesmen, living in the midst of of the people, with whom is lodged the final power to adopt the measure, as it has already been done in the Free States and in the old Spanish colonies.

Though I could not acquiesce in the opinion of Mrs. Mott, that the abolition of slavery should be preached in season and out of season, by the defender of the rights of nations, I yet fell beneath the charm of her moral superiority, and I warmly wished that I could spend hours, to listen and to discuss with her and Mr. Mott, in the attractive circle of her children and grandchildren. Great was, therefore, my astonishment, when, upon my expressing my admiration for Mrs. Mott to some gentlemen, one of them exclaimed, " You do not mean to say, that you have called on that lady ?"

" Of course I have, was my answer; why should I not ?—I am most gratified to have done so, and I only regret that the shortness of the time we have to spend here, prevents me from often repeating my visit."

" But she is a furious Abolitionist," retorted the gentleman.—" It will do great harm to Governor Kossuth, if you associate with that party."

" I perceive, sir,"—said I—" that you highly estimate Mrs. Mott, as you consider her alone a whole party. But if any friend of Governor Kossuth, even if he himself converses with a person who has strong opinions against slavery, what harm can there be in that?"

"Your cause will then lose many friends in this city," was the answer.

I was perfectly amazed at such intolerance, and expressed this frankly. The gentleman, however, attempted to point out to me what mischief the Abolitionists were doing, and how long ago emancipation would have been carried in all the States, had the Abolitionists not so violently interfered; and besides (continued he) Mrs. Mott preaches!

" Well," replied I, " do not many Quaker ladies preach occasionally?"

This fact was admitted, but another gentleman remarked, that Mrs. Mott was dangerous, as her sermons were powerfully inciting.

" Is she perhaps a fighting Quaker," enquired I, " who appeals to the words of the Saviour, that he did not come to send peace on earth, but the sword?"

" I am a fighting Quaker myself," said the gentleman; " my forefathers fought in the revolutionary war, but Mrs. Mott is a Hicksite."

To my enquiry, what were the tenets of the Hicksites inspiring such dislike, I got the answer, " They are very bad, very bad; they, in fact, believe nothing."

This assertion was so contradictory to the impression left on my mind by Mrs. Mott, that I attentively perused some of her sermons, and I found them pervaded by that fervent desire to seek truth and to do right, of which Jesus teaches us that blessed are they which do hunger and thirst after righteousness, for they shall be filled—and therefore, although my views differ from hers on many points, I perceived that party-feeling must be strong in Philadelphia, to arouse such unjust views as I had heard expressed, and I could not help thinking that the meddling and narrow spirit had not yet departed here, which, in 1707, proposed that young men should be obliged to marry at a certain age, and that only two sorts of clothes should be worn, one kind for summer, and one for winter.

As I later learnt, the Hicksites got their name from Elias Hicks, a celebrated preacher of the Society of Friends, who taught doctrines of Unitarian character, and got a considerable influence amongst the Quakers, which led to a disruption of this peaceful community. About three hundred congregations called themselves orthodox, and gave up communion with the other two hundred congregations, whom they since designate as Hicksites.

Dec. 26th.—We visited the large prison established on the plan of solitary confinement. The strong wall which surrounds it, and the heavy gate, opening on its court, give, even at first sight, the appalling

impression of forcible and complete isolation. To be
utterly shut out from nature, shut out from intercourse with fellow-man! there is something terrific
in this idea; and still more so, if we consider that
the secluded culprit is alone with the conscience of
his crime. A gentleman who accompanied us told
me, that the criminal is always blindfolded when he
is first led to these precincts, that he may not make
out to which part of the building he is taken.

When I entered the corridors, with the long rows
of cells, strongly barred, I felt as if surrounded by
tombs;—all was silent, motionless. I experienced,
therefore, a kind of pleasant surprise when the bars
were withdrawn, to behold, not skeletons, but rather
healthy-looking persons. We visited several cells, and
I spoke with every prisoner to whom we went, because I thought that it must be a privilege to these
poor people to speak, as they are so rarely allowed to
do it. They likewise seemed to enjoy it, except one
black man, who appeared to have lost the use of his
tongue, and though he did not look bewildered at
our intrusion, he answered our questions only by
nodding his head.

Most of the women whom I saw, readily told the
melancholy tale of their errors, and some of them
said it was a comfort to be granted reflection on their
sins; others bewailed their fate with tears, though
they all admitted that they were very well kept. The
cells seemed to me considerably more spacious and
far less gloomy than at Pentonville. In England,

where the lodging and the food of the poorest class
is wretched, the prison-rule cannot grant any comfort to the prisoner, lest the penitentiary become
more attractive than the poor-house. In America
the poorer classes live more comfortably; the prison,
therefore, can also be less dreary, the seclusion is the
principal means of expiation. Some of the small
rooms, occupied by females, I found ornamented with
little pictures and flowers. Books I met with everywhere,—Bibles, chapters of religious meditation,
travels, history. The library is ample enough, and
is kept in good order by one of the prisoners, a
poorly-looking elderly man, who was sentenced for
forgery. This crime, and theft and larceny, appear
the most common.

Dec. 27th.—Independence Hall, where Kossuth
was received, is for ever memorable as the place where
the continental Congress declared the Independence
of America, and carried on the war and government
during the most trying days of the struggle. At
present it is used by the District Court of the United
States, and by the City Courts. It is a stately brick
building, one story high, nine windows broad, adorned
by two columns at the door, and surmounted by a
steeple in the periwig style. It was built about 1730,
intended for the use of the provincial assemblies of
Pennsylvania, but the republican spirit of the colonies
was already then alive, and the ancient bell in the
belfry, cast in Philadelphia long before the revolution,

bears the inscription,—" Proclaim liberty throughout the land, and to all the people thereof."

The declaration of Independence, adopted on the 4th of July, 1776, was signed in the lower hall of the building on the 6th. It was done, not in a fit of enthusiasm, but after mature consideration. Massachusetts and Virginia took the lead, but the middle States, Delaware, New York, and the Jerseys, were not yet ripe for bidding adieu to British connexion, their delegates did sign the document but several days later. They were already in actual war with England; blood had flowed, and yet there were many who wavered, and did not like to express with pen and ink, what the sword and musket had declared already in letters of blood. But John Hancock, of Massachusetts, signed his name in a large strong hand, and rising from his seat, said, "There! John Bull can read my name without spectacles, and may now double his reward of £500 for my head. That is my defiance." And Charles Carroll, of Maryland, put the aristocratic designation "of Carrolton" after his name, that amongst the many Carrolls, there should be no mistake about the signer of the Independence. On the 8th of July, the document was read from a platform before the hall, to the assembled masses, and the bell of the steeple "proclaimed liberty throughout the land." When Lafayette visited America, fifty years after the declaration, the historical hall was to be his hall of audience, and duly to honour " *the nation's guest;*" all the former

historical decorations and furniture were taken away by
the committee of reception, and the room was fitted up
with French tapestry and modern mahogany furniture !
It was in this hall, that the second guest of the nation,
Kossuth, was greeted by the authorities, and delivered
his address to the people of Philadelphia.

II. GREAT MEN OF PHILADELPHIA.

Stephen Girard, at the time of his death (1831)
the second wealthiest man in the United States, and
by his memorable will the great benefactor of Philadelphia, is a singular instance of the way in which
money sometimes is acquired and enjoyed in North
America.   Born near Bordeaux, in 1750, he left
France at the age of ten, as a cabin boy, bound to the
West Indies, whence he proceeded to New York, and
sailed for some years between that city, New Orleans,
and the West Indies, as cabin-boy, sailor, mate, and
eventually master and owner.   He went largely into
the St. Domingo trade, and a brig and schooner of his
were lying at Cap Française, when the great revolt of
the negroes occurred.   Many planters removed their
valuables on board of his vessels, but few only of
them escaped from the wholesale butchery of the
white population.   Whole families perished, and Mr.
Girard could never discover the heirs of the greatest
part of the wealth, about 50,000 dollars, which thus
remained in his hands.   Having acquired an immense
fortune in the East Indian trade, and by banking

speculations, he died in December, 1831. He always had been homely in his dress and personal appearance, his furniture was of the plainest kind, his equipage an old chaise and a common nag. He indulged in no amusements; his marriage was unhappy, on account of the asperity of his temper; his only child died in infancy; he had no one whom he loved as a friend. He had no sympathies for individuals, but only for the masses; for future generations, not for the present. He never was moved to charity by tales of distress, but he did not idolize gold, nor did he spend it for his own gratification, but it was his delight to see it usefully employed. A young man who had opened a store in a neighbouring village, requested him for some wares on credit, though he could not offer any security. Girard asked him how he intended to carry the wares to the village. " On my back," said the shopkeeper. Girard was pleased with the answer: he gave him the wares, and three dollars besides, in order to hire a donkey for the conveyance of the parcel. But the trader said, he could make better use of the money in his business, took the parcel on his back, and went on. When shortly afterwards he returned to Philadelphia to pay his debt, Girard opened with him a large credit, saying, that this man deserves support, and must become rich. In result, by the aid of the eccentric Frenchman and his own energies, he did become a rich man.

Another time he encouraged Samuel Coates, a shrewd Quaker, to call on him next day for some aid

needed by the Pennsylvania Hospital, saying that if
he chanced to find him *on the right footing,* he might
give something.   Samuel came at breakfast time.
" Well, what have you come for, Samuel?"   " Any
thing thee pleases, Stephen."   Girard gave him a
check for 200 dollars, which Samuel stuffed into his
pocket without looking at it.   " What! you do not
look at the check I gave you?"   " No, Stephen, beg-
gars must not be choosers."   " Hand me back the
check again," demanded Girard.   " No, no, Stephen;
a bird in the hand is worth two in the bush."   " By
George!" exclaimed Girard, "you have caught me
on the right footing."   He then drew a check for 500
dollars ; and, presenting it to Mr. Coates, asked him
to look at it.   " Well, to please thee, Stephen, I will."
" Now, give me back the first check," demanded
Girard, which was instantly complied with.   Few
understood him, however, so well as Samuel Coates.
A Baptist clergyman, to whom he gave 200 dollars
in the same way for a church, made a remark con-
cerning his ability to give much more.   " Let me
look at the check," said Girard.   It was handed to
him, and he tore it up with indigation.*

Of his immense wealth, estimated variously at from
six to twelve million dollars, he bequeathed a few
very moderate legacies to his relatives; to the city of
New Orleans, for sanitary purposes, and measures for
promoting public health, a considerable amount of

* 'Historical Collection of the State of Pennsylvania.'   By
Sherman Day.

real estate in Louisiana; to the State of Pennsylvania 300,000 dollars, to be expended in internal improvements by canal navigation, the said sum not to be paid unless the laws be passed by the Pennsylvania legislature, required to carry out several clauses of the will. The great bulk of his fortune he bestowed upon the city of Philadelphia, in trust: 500,000 dollars to be expended in opening, widening, and improving a street along the Delaware; sundry residuary sums to the hospital, other public charities, and the promotion of the health and comfort of the inhabitants; and, as his great and favourite object, 2,000,000 dollars, or more if necessary, to build and endow a college for the education of "poor white male orphans," as many as the said income shall be adequate to maintain, to be received between the ages of six and ten, and to be bound out between the ages of fourteen and eighteen, to suitable occupations, as those of agriculture, navigation, arts, mechanical trades, and manufactures. The following injunctions are extracted from the will:—

"The orphans admitted into the college shall be there fed with plain but wholesome food, clothed with plain but decent apparel (no distinctive dress ever to be worn), and lodged in a plain but safe manner. Due regard shall be paid to their health, and to this end their persons and clothes shall be kept clean, and they shall have suitable and rational exercise and recreation. They shall be instructed in the various branches of a sound education, comprehending reading, writing, grammar, arithmetic, geography, navigation, surveying, practical mathematics, astronomy, natural, chemical, and experimental philosophy, the French and Spanish languages (I do not forbid, but I do not recommend the Greek and Latin languages) ; and such other learning and science as the capacities of the several scholars may merit or · warrant. I would have them taught facts and things, rather than words or signs. And, especially, I desire that, by every proper means, a pure attachment to our Republican institutions, and to the sacred rights of conscience, as guaranteed by our happy institutions, shall be formed and fostered in the minds of the scholars.

"I enjoin and require, that no ecclesiastic, missionary, or minister, of any sect whatever, shall ever hold or exercise any station or duty whatever in the said college; nor shall any such person ever be admitted, for any purpose, or as a visitor, within the premises appropriated to the purposes of the said college. In making this restriction, I do not mean to cast any reflection upon any sect or person whatsoever; but, as there is such a multitude of sects, and such a diversity of opinion amongst them, I desire to keep the tender minds of the orphans, who are to derive advantage from this bequest, free from the excitement which clashing doctrines and sectarian controversy are so apt to produce: my desire is, that all the instructors and teachers in the college shall take pains to instil into the minds of the scholars the purest principles of morality, so that, on their entrance into active life, they may, from inclination and habit, evince benevolence towards their fellow-creatures, and a love of truth, sobriety, and industry, —adopting, at the same time, such religious tenets as their matured reason may enable them to prefer."

When Mrs. Pulszky visited Girard's college, she was struck by the palace-like appearance of the buildings and the sumptuousness of the apartments. Girard's will, which enjoined "to avoid needless ornament," has not been strictly adhered to, and the expenditure, in this respect, has retarded the opening of the institution from the time of the death of the founder in 1831 till 1848. It appeared to her also, that the desire of Mr. Girard, to have them taught facts and things, should also be extended to their practical education. She found them too much attended on; they have not even to take care of their wardrobe themselves, but there is a special person appointed not only to take care of its repair, but like-wise to keep the clothes nicely folded up, and placed in good order. Children cannot be early enough accustomed to attend to their own wants, especially these orphan-boys, who, having attained their six-teenth year, are thrown into the world upon their own energies, unprovided by the institution, in which they have been for ten years brought up in a most liberal way, as the subjoined figures show:

In 1849, there were 205 orphans in the school. The appropriation for clothing was 5000 dollars, for subsistence 11,500 dollars, fuel 2000 dollars, furniture 1000 dollars. In 1850, for 305 scholars, clothing 9900 dollars, subsistence 17,000 dollars, fuel 2200 dollars, furniture 5000 dollars. But it may be premature to express an opinion on the management of this institution, which until now has established only the preliminary classes, adding every year a new one, until the intentions of the founder are fulfilled.

The names of two great men are blended with Philadelphia, thongh they do not belong exclusively either to the city, or even to America,—the names of William Penn, and of Benjamin Franklin. William Penn, the "proprietor" of Pennsylvania, the founder of Philadelphia, is naturally judged in America from a different point of view than in Europe. For the New World he is not the courtier of the Stuarts, but the great statesman, the founder of a new political commonwealth, untrammelled by the intrigues of a corrupt court, which protected his principles of religious equality only because they were to be the back-door for introducing Roman Catholicism by stealth into England. In America Penn had no obligations towards the crown, and had not to take a conniving, compromising, wavering position, between the despotic tendencies of the Stuarts and the passive resistance of the corporations and of the people. Penn comes to his colony with the determination to embody all the noble aspirations of his soul. He is as fond of the Indians as only Rousseau could have been; he brings to them the simple message of peace and love, " the English and the Indians shall respect the same moral law, shall be alike secure in their pursuits and their possessions, and adjust every difference by a peaceful tribunal, composed of an equal number from each race." He describes them quite in a sentimental way. " In liberality," he says, " they excel; nothing is too good for their friend; give them a fine gun, coat, or other thing, it may pass twenty hands before it sticks; light of heart;— strong affections but soon spent;—the most merry creatures that live;—feast and dance perpetually. They never have much, nor want much; wealth circulates like the blood; all parts partake, and though none shall want what another has, yet exact observers of property. They care for little because they want but little, and the reason is,—a little contents them. In this they are sufficiently revenged on us; if they are ignorant of our pleasures, they are also free from our pains. We sweat and toil to live; their pleasure feeds them, I mean their hunting, fishing, and fowling, and this table is spread everywhere." Are not these extracts from Penn's letter, to the Free Society of Traders, like a dream of a poet? He did not yet understand the hunter, nor surmise his unavoidable collision with the agriculturists. He meets King Tammany under the elm-tree, and signs there the treaty of alliance and brotherhood. He buys the land of them, and " makes" a chain of friendship between the Red and the White, which should always be made stronger and stronger, and kept bright and clear, without rust or spot, between their children and children's children.

As to the Whites, their charter is the charter of political liberty, of religious equality, and he has every reason to congratulate himself upon his success. When he leaves Philadelphia, there is as yet no Indian difficulty, no party-feud in Pennsylvania. His colony thrives and prospers. His farewell letter to it is a touching evidence of his affection and hopes for the small commonwealth he had founded.

"My love and life is to you and with you, and no water can quench it, nor distance wear it out, or bring it to an end. I have been with you, cared over you, and served you with unfeigned love, and you are beloved of me, and near to me, beyond utterance. .... And thou *Philadelphia*, the virgin settlement of this Province, named before thou wert born, what love, what care, what service, and what travail has there been to bring thee forth! Oh, that thou mayest be kept from the evil that would overwhelm thee; that, faithful to the God of thy mercies, in the life of righteousness, thou mayest be preserved to the end. My soul prays to God for thee, that thou mayest stand in the day of trial, that thy children may be blessed of the Lord, and thy people saved by His power."

But Penn's hopes were not fulfilled. For the welfare of his colony he had struggled for years in England, and now he could not earn the fruits of his toils. Quarrels between the colonists of different creeds, bickerings between the legislative and executive, and pecuniary embarrassments, embittered his later years. The change of dynasty in England, and the jealousy of the crown against the Proprietary governments in America, encouraged his enemies; the jurisdiction of his province was wrested from him by the crown, and though he was reinstated, and returned to the colony, he had again to go to England, in order to prevent the Proprietor's administration from being changed into Royal government. He could not remain on the place of his predilection, for which he had sacrificed everything, and all his plans for peace on earth, and good-will towards men, remained unsuccessful in the colony, as well as in England; though an affectionate patriarchal relation subsisted between Penn and his province until his death, in spite of the endless colonial quarrels and feuds.

But his family had not inherited his benevolence; they took their proprietory and feudal privileges only for a source of income, and, so soon as in 1764, John Penn, the grandson of William, by proclamation, offered bounties for the capture or scalps of Indians !* The American revolution swept away the feudal titles of Penn's family, but his benevolence, and the charter which he framed, are always recorded with gratitude and admiration by the people of Pennsylvania, though

* 'Historical Collections of Pennsylvania,' by Sherman Day, p. 29, from Gordon, p. 438.

the frequent riots in Philadelphia prove but too strongly, that it is only by name, and not in fact, the city of brotherly love.   Still Penn's spirit lives in the public institutions for the moral and physical care of the poor, in the almshouses, hospitals, prisons, and colleges.

There are very few men whose example and writings had a more powerful influence on their people, than Benjamin Franklin.   In many respects, his personal character has become the character of the Americans, of three parts of the Union out of four.   Rising to consideration by hard work, sobriety, and industry; calculating and abiding his time in politics; a keen observer of the physical as well as of the moral world; a little vain of his own morality, at least as far as never to put his light under the bushel; proud of his country, not caring for Europe, and yet gratified by all the flattery bestowed on him in Europe; benevolent in life and unrelenting in polemics,—he is the prototype of many distinguished Americans.   He had perhaps less faith in the triumph of American Independence than the Massachusetts Republicans; he advises his friends at the time of the stamp-tax, " to light up the candles of industry and economy, as the sun of liberty has set;" and he would have acceded to every honourable compromise with the mother country; but when the Revolution actually broke out, he served the cause of liberty with unflinching patriotism.   He liked to measure things by convenience, and his answer to Thomas Paine, about the proposed publication of his 'Age of Reason,' characterises him admirably. " I would advise you," he wrote, " not to attempt unchaining the tiger, but to burn the piece before it is seen by any other person. If men are so wicked *with religion,* what would they be *without it ?*"

There is yet one name which should be recorded by every visitor of Philadelphia, the name of Robert Morris, whose biography reminds us of the life of the heroes of Cornelius Nepos. Born in Lancashire, brought by his emigrant father to America, entering into commercial business in Philadelphia, he became one of the leading merchants of that city. But his business and his pecuniary interests did not slacken his patriotism ; he cordially entered into the non-importation agreements which preceded the war, and courageously affixed his name to the Declaration of Independence. During the war, the financial difficulties of the United States were not less formidable than the armies of England, and whilst Washington had the more glorious task of carrying on the war on the battle-field, Robert Morris, who was entrusted with the management of the finances, had to provide for army ammunition, sulphur, saltpetre, lead, provisions, and accoutrements ; he had to fit out a naval armament, to negociate bills of exchange, and to procure foreign loans. His own credit stood often higher than that of his country, and he never hesitated to pledge it for the public necessities. It was owing to him that the decisive operations of

1781 were not completely defeated from the want of supplies, and when the currency was depreciated, it was against him that all the complaints were directed. His merits were not less important, though less conspicuous, than those of the generals who defeated the English, or of the statesmen who negociated the treaties and framed the constitution.

But it was not his lot to enjoy the freedom for which he had toiled so hard and so successfully. He had expended his wealth for his country in her hour of need, but in her prosperity she forsook him. Involved in land speculations and building schemes, he broke down, and in his last years he was confined in prison for debt.

III. BALTIMORE.

(From Mrs. Pulszky's Diary.)

Dec. 27th.—The trip from Philadelphia to Baltimore, is so shortened by the railway, that though we left the Quaker city after breakfast, we should have arrived at Baltimore in good season for dinner, if we could have proceeded from the terminus straight to the hotel. But a numerous military escort, and manifold associations, with a whole exhibition of banners, obstructed our way, and though we turned into a bye street to avoid the throng, the crowds were so dense on all points, that we took a couple of hours to reach the Eutaw House, where apartments had been prepared for us.

The city gives the impression of sprightly gaiety;
the red brick houses look cheerfully on a boisterous
population, moving to and fro in the streets, with
quick movements and animated looks. None but
the coloured people loiter about the corners of the
avenues, staring idly with their large, dazzling dark
eyes, and walking lazily but a few steps to stop and
stare again. The negro women look less drowsy;
they cluster together, talking and glancing around,
obviously delighted at the pageantry,—the topic of
the day. They form the gaudiest portion of the
varied objects before us; their dress, though poor in
material, is of brilliant hue; none wears a dark shirt,
or a sable handkerchief; all are adorned with purple,
yellow, and blue. These groups give a Southern
aspect to the city, in spite of the masses of snow and
ice, accumulated along the paths cleared for the procession.

But it is not only the black population which
impart so peculiar a stamp to Baltimore; its citizens,
too, and especially its ladies, are decidedly different
from those I met in the Northern States. The gentlemen here, I found in general warmer and gayer in
their conversation than the grave Philadelphians, and
more communicative than the ever busily preoccupied
inhabitants of New York. They appear to care less
and enjoy more. Nevertheless, their physiognomies
are marked in a certain degree, by the shrewdness of
the commercial Anglo-Saxon race.

I had repeatedly heard in the States, that the ladies

of Baltimore were exquisitely beautiful, and I found
that they justify that assertion; they unite, in some
measure, the charms of the North and of the South;
the dazzling skin and the rich hair; the brilliant hue
of the eyes and the ruby lips; the stately deportment,
the graceful movements. There is much vivacity in
their appearance and in their language; they seem
very fond of music, and have the credit of singing
and playing very well; their society is most pleasant.

The prison, I visited here, left a dismal impression
on my mind.

Though the "Auburn" system is adopted, and,
in consequence, the prisoners are not isolated, but
working together in different shops, they look, on the
whole, much more blunted than in Philadelphia. I
think that this may, in part, be owing to the insufficient
ventilation all over the building, and, more especially,
to the closeness of the dark, low, and small cells in
which the culprits are locked up, after their day's
work is done.

I perceived a little black boy of about eleven years,
and I asked him why, and for how long he had been
sentenced. "For life," was the answer. "This is
awful, how is it possible!?" exclaimed I. I then
was told that this unnatural hapless being had broken
the skull of another child with whom he played,
because he would not give him up his toy; that it
was ascertained at the time, that when he committed
the deed, he was fully aware that death was painful

and irretrievably destructive. But it seemed to me
monstrous, that a child is sentenced to prison for
life, instead of being sent to a house of correction.
Doomed to endless prison at the age of eleven ! public
revenge instead of education ! The law which dic-
tates such treatment, does not seem in accordance
with the institutions of the United States.

Dec. 28th.—Of the public monuments of Baltimore,
and especially of the Washington column, I think it
may be said, that they less adorn the city than the
city adorns them. Their white marble, forms a
pleasant contrast to the surrounding red buildings,
but they are rather historical monuments than monuments of art. Is it not remarkable that the custom
of putting statues at the top of columns, where
nobody can see their workmanship, which was introduced by the later Roman Emperors, has been
imitated in London and Paris, and even across the
Atlantic ? Our artists cannot vie with the taste of
the Greeks ; therefore we content ourselves to imitate
the costly productions of the declining Empire.
Verily, if the public monuments of our days should
once be considered as tests of our civilisation,—our
glory will be small !

CHAPTER V.

WASHINGTON CITY.

I. SOCIETY.

(From Mrs. Pulszky's Diary.)

When on the 30th of December we reached Washington, the fog was as dense and as yellow, as if it had been freshly imported from London. The first man who greeted us at the railway terminus was Mr. Seward, late governor of New York, now senator for that State,—one of the three gentlemen appointed by Congress to receive Kossuth. He made a most agreeable impression on me. His appearance is distinguished;—a noble forehead, light grey hair, penetrating eyes, pointed New English features, in which shrewdness and benevolence are blended; his elegant dress and easy manners convey at once the idea, that he is at home in the drawing-room as well as in the senate. His conversation is fluent and instructive, fascinating even to his political opponents. I had repeated opportunity of seeing that this gentleman, the heir of John Quincy Adams's principles and views, did in fact reconcile, by his personal amiability, all those Southerners who came in personal contact with him. Senator Seward, though by the unceasing denunciations of the 'New York Herald,' he is the

bugbear of the South, is yet highly respected by
Southern statesmen, and has never become an object
of those violent parliamentary attacks, with which
John Quincy Adams, in spite of his eminent services
as Ambassador, Secretary of State, and President,
was assailed, when, towards the close of his remarkable career, he again entered Congress as a member
of the house.

Senator Seward is the most influential of the Whig
leaders. He has the instinct of the future, and
never shrinks from taking up measures, because they
are unpopular, if he foresees that in time they will
get the majority. When we arrived in America, his
popularity was at an ebb, for he was known as un-
friendly to the fugitive slave law; but before we left
the United States, he had won back the majority
amongst the Whigs, and commanded the esteem of
the Democrats.

We had hardly entered the drawing-room of
Brown's Hotel, when the Secretary of State was announced. The countenance of Mr. Webster is well
known in England. The vast bald forehead, the
broad thick black eyebrows over the stern large
dark eyes, the reserved countenance, the emphatic
deep voice, the measured gait, impart a gravity to his
demeanour, extended to every one of his movements,
even to the cool hand-shaking with which he greets
you. He was evidently surprised at Kossuth's mild,
melancholy, dignified manner. The unmoveable
countenance of the silencious Secretary of State was

lighted up for a moment, when he first beheld the oriental solemnity of the great Hungarian: he remembered, perhaps, the sunny time of his own manhood, when he was the warm advocate of struggling Greece. The cold statesman, the logical expounder of the interests of the United States, was ever open to noble impulses; but his calculating mind controlled the impressions of his heart. He had perhaps expected to meet in Kossuth a visionary agitator, a theoretical revolutionist; but a short interview obviously satisfied him of Kossuth's superiority. A few days later he was asked, how he liked the ' nation's guest.' " He has the manners of a king; his is a royal nature," was the answer.

General Cass, and General Shields, the members of the reception-committee of the Senate, were our next visitors.

The old explorer of the head-waters of the Mississippi, the celebrated ambassador at the court of Louis Philippe, the most popular of the democratic leaders, has one resemblance in his fortunes with the Whig Secretary of State—he has not been able to attain the highest position in his country, though inferior men have attained it.

It is indeed remarkable, that, for a series of years, the most prominent political men of both parties, Henry Clay, Webster, Calhoun, Cass, Buchanan, were not elected Presidents. They were all ministers; but a prominent parliamentary career and a high rank among the statesmen, is in America conducive

to renown and respect, not to popularity. Military
chiefs and statesmen of second order have more
chances at the presidential elections. The masses
require instinctively a stout heart and sound common
sense in their chief, and they wish to see him sur-
sounded by the men of first-rate talent, as his advisers,
at the head of the departments. Democracy never
did, and never does, think it safe to entrust the
supreme power to men of genius, though it requires
their exertions for the public weal.

General Cass, tall and stout, full of vivacity and
French politeness to the ladies, strikes by the frankness and cordiality of his manners.

General James Shields, the democratic senator of
Illinois, is a " self-made" man. An Irish emigrant,
he became a lawyer of influence in the West, and
took a prominent part in the Mexican war, at the
head of a regiment of volunteers. Bold and gallant,
as his countrymen used to be, he distinguished himself in different battles, and when severely wounded,
he attracted the general interest of his adopted
country; so prominent and attractive had been his
gallantry. His physiognomy is very pleasant. Dark
hair, dark brown eyes, dark complexion, lively
demeanour and conversation, elegant manners and
eloquence, recall his origin; acuteness and precision
in expression, comprehensive liberal views, unpre-
judiced research, were developed in his character on
the free soil of America. Let those who revile the
Irish as *Celts*, go to America for a different reply !

"Don't you go to the President to-morrow?" was repeatedly said to me on the last of December. "No, I am not invited," answered I. "Well, nobody is asked, and everybody is expected; it is a levee," was the reply—"all Washington will be there, and many people come in from Georgetown and the neighbourhood."

I then understood that the levee lasted the whole morning, and consisted in a drawing-room review on a very large scale, as hundreds and hundreds of people defiled before the President. I little expected that we were ourselves to have a second edition of this New-Year's day ceremony.

Coming from the President, the visitors thronged to Brown's Hotel, to claim an introduction to Kossuth; and as they were considerably more than our apartment could hold, we could neither request them to sit down, nor, of course, would we keep them standing; therefore we had no choice but to bow and to shake hands, without attempting any conversation. Yet there was a great deal of variety in this pantomimic intercourse. One moment a lady trips in, wrapped in velvet and furs from head to foot, a fan in her hand, her uplifted veil flowing down over her plumed bonnet. The gentleman who accompanies her, proclaims her name: I mumble, "most happy indeed;" we look at each other; we both bow; the top of her fingers lightly touches my hand;—she passes on. An old senator follows, he emphatically presses Madame Kossuth's hand, saying, "Welcome to our

shores." Next a lady, in a rather weather-beaten
morning attire, with a shawl and bonnet, that must
have witnessed many a New Year's-day levee; she
stares at us most intently, and only utters, " How do
you do?" I re-echo her salutation; she stares again,
and most probably would long continue to do so, but
she is pushed on by another lady, looking very determined, with several children at her side and at her
heels. " Take off your hat, Charley!" says she, to
discipline her son. The children, behind her, cry,
" We can't see;" a little confusion ensues. The
lady elbows right and left; " Now the girls can see,"
exclaims she; and begins to enquire, how many
children Madame Kossuth has, and how many I, and
where they are, and how they are, poor little things!
But the gentleman who has the trying task of introductions, gets impatient, and exclaims: " This will
not do; please, ladies and gentlemen, to pass on; so
many are coming; please, ladies, not to stop."—And
ladies and gentlemen, old and young, pass now in so
quick succession, that I can hardly retain the name
or the faces, though many of them are well worth
remembering; members of the Senate; generals and
colonels; officers of the navy and their ladies; interesting and sweet countenances from the North and
the South, the East and the West. Here we meet
with no bureaucratical type of civil officers, and with
no stiffly trained military deportment, such as form
the main bulk of the visitors at levees on the continent of Europe; nor is there the slightest trace of

the stately splendour of the aristocratical mother-
country; nor yet is there the monotony of the conventional drawing-room dress-coat and cravat, for
every one comes as suits his occupation, his habit,
or his convenience; in gold-embroidered regimentals,
in a paletôt or in Oxonians, in a white cravat or a
knitted shawl twisted round his neck, in kid gloves
or without gloves.   On the whole I may affirm, that
Mr. N. P. Willis, the American chronicler of European
dandyism, has not yet made many disciples in the
United States.

The room begins to grow emptier, a few visitors
yet approach, amongst them a lovely woman.   She
has tears in her eyes as she welcomes us to the land
of the free; she leads in her hand a little girl of striking beauty, who wistfully glances up to us, and her
mother says: "Darling, these are the ladies of whom
you have heard so often, the ladies who have suffered
so much with their children, should you not like to
have likewise the dear little ones with us?"

Such warm greeting we had repeatedly experienced
in every quarter of the States which we had visited;
at the firesides of the rich, amidst the crowds of the
people; in the shops of the working-classes, in the
asylum of the blind.   But that tearful sympathy,
freely expressed likewise in the drawing-room, deeply
impressed me with the conviction, that artificial con-
ventionalism has here not deadened that delightful
sensibility, whose absence leaves so many fashionable
resorts void of every genuine charm.

On the 6th of January we dined at the White House, the official abode of the President. Every one who is familiar with European "etiquette," and its traditional influence, must wonder how utterly every vestige of this kind has disappeared across the ocean. It is true that in Europe too, Spain perhaps excepted, etiquette has, since the first French Revolution, ceased to be what it is still in the East, *a code of the formalities of reverence*, whose laws are strictly enforced by education, and are religiously observed by habit. There the difference of rank and of age is not only marked by the difference of title, of ornaments, and of seats, but persons are distinctly honoured by every movement with which they are greeted, by every gesture with which they are met, and which, therefore, convey a symbolical meaning. In Europe such ceremonial has been superseded by a conventional rule of the style of dress and the order of precedency at official occasions; and though these offer but a vague historical interest, their pomp and regularity has a certain effect of solemnity. At the White House there is nothing of the kind to be seen. There are here no pictures, no statues, no silk tapestry, no costly furniture, scarcely a few prints, and even these are presents of the French artist who engraved them. The appearance of the guests of the President is as simple as his abode. This formed one of the topics of my conversation with the President, whose neighbour I was at table. He remarked that the people of the United States claimed economy in every detail from their chief magistrate, and that on one occasion, when an ex-President stood up for the Presidency, his opponents used the argument against him, that he had introduced gilded spoons and elegant plate at the White House. Here it is only the intrinsic dignity of the personal character which can invest the President with social authority. We read of Washington,* " that he received visitors with a dignified bow, in a manner avoiding to shake hands, even with his best friends." But it certainly required the acknowledged superiority of " the father of the nation," that public opinion did not protest against such reserve; for to meet every one on terms of perfect equality, is the right and the custom of every American citizen.

Mr. Fillmore has, in his countenance and in his manners, an expression of natural kind-hearted frankness, fully in harmony with that principle : and Mrs. Fillmore resembles him in that respect. Their daughter has likewise imbibed this republican characteristic, and she unites with it an amiable sincerity, which struck me, when I remarked to her how very well she spoke French; on which she answered to me, that she had had opportunity to practise it in the school where she lately had been a teacher. Such views, fostered and maintained by public opinion,— the absence of all military pageantry in the dress and the household of the President, though he is the commander-in-chief of the army, navy, and militia,—

* Watson's Annals of Philadelphia.

is an insurmountable barrier against any thought of
usurpation, and even the hand-shaking with everybody,—the most tiresome of all the Presidential
duties,—has become one of the great guarantees of
the republican institutions. It retains the chief
magistrate on the level of the citizen, reminding him
incessantly that he is but one of them. And therefore it is not so painful for a President to return to
private life as we should imagine. On the 3d of
March, four years after his election, he removes
quietly to a hotel in Washington, and having settled
his domestic affairs, he again takes up his former
profession. Jefferson goes to his plantation; John
Quincy Adams recommences his political career, as
member of the house of representatives; Tyler
accepts a small municipal office in Virginia; and
Mr. Fillmore will probably return to the office, where
his junior partner has, during the time of his Presidency, conducted his law business.

The most remarkable of the guests for me, besides
those whom I knew already, were the President of
the Senate, Senator King, of Alabama, who has since
been elected Vice-President of the United States,
General Scott, the commander-in-chief, the hero of
the Mexican war, and Mr. Kane, the young naturalist,
who had accompanied the embassy of Mr. Everett to
China, and lately the Arctic Expedition, which Mr.
Grinell, of New York, fitted out in search of Sir
John Franklin.

General Scott, tall, bulky, and commanding in his appearance, is as prolix in his words as he is concise in his actions.   One of those great captains who never lost a battle, he has repeated the exploits of Cortez.   With a small force, chiefly of volunteers, he has taken the fortress of Vera Cruz, fought his way against fearful odds, from the low land to the plateau of Mexico, defeated the splendid army of the Mexicans led by Santa Anna, who was styled the Napoleon of the West, and has conquered with ten thousand men, the halls of Montezuma.   And yet this hero is no friend of war.   During the excitement of the Canadian insurrection, when the loyalists had destroyed the steamboat Caroline, in American waters, and slain American sympathisers, nothing but the discretion and firm conduct of General Scott, who held the command in those parts, averted a war with England.   A remarkable proof of his disinterestedness, and of his patriotism, was given by him, when in Mexico the most influential citizens requested him to remain there as head of their Republic, and offered him, in this case, a great pecuniary reward, for they said he alone would be able to govern well the disturbed commonwealth.   But the General rejected this offer, he never would give up his proud position of a citizen of the United States, not even for a Presidential chair in Mexico.   He is one of the living glories of the United States,—in his private life as pure and unstained as in his public career.

As most of the fashionable people at Washington reside in hotels and boarding-houses, to spare the trouble and expense of temporary establishments; balls and crowded parties in private houses can but rarely take place. In consequence, the "Washington Assemblies," balls on subscription, directed by a committee of the leading gentlemen of the society, are considered the most pleasant and elegant resorts of amusement. One entertainment of this kind was given during our stay there. The aspect of the Washington assemblies is like that of the elegant subscription balls in the capitals of Germany, which, though exclusive by the nature of their arrangement, yet assemble more different circles of society, than we meet at the routs of a private house. The Friday levees of the President, during the season, are mere abridgments of the great New Year's Day levee. The door of the President is open to every American citizen.

A party of Indians, from the far West, had arrived in Washington, with complaints and petitions to their " great father."

The President invited us to witness the audience in the White House. The chiefs and braves of four different tribes were here, and two of them had brought their squaws along with them; clad in their skins and blankets, or ornamented with feather crowns, with their clubs and pipes, crouching on the floor, they offered a most picturesque scene. They were really red, that is to say, they were *painted;* but, when washed, the red man is by no means red, but light-brown.

Mr. Fillmore, sitting in an arm-chair, surrounded by some of the government officials and the Indian agents, addressed his red children in the usual way, summoning them to explain the object of their visit. He did it with a dignity which struck me as different from his usual demeanour. The communications were made through several native interpreters, as the Indians did not all speak the same language. The chiefs rose one after the other, shook hands with their " great father," and complained that the emigrants to California were incessantly crossing their hunting-grounds, with horses and waggons, frightening away the deer, without giving compensation for the damage; that they had but small stores of Indian corn; that they feared starvation, and requested redress of their " great father."

One of the chiefs, an Otoe, mentioned that their tribe never had raised the tomahawk against their white brethren, and yet they were perishing, like the others. Another chief found that Washington was so far from the Rocky Mountains, that he wished to get a horse to ride back. They all looked very cunning and shrewd. They belonged to entirely savage tribes, not yet settled in the " Indian territory;" but were the original owners of their hunting-grounds.

The "great father" told them that the Indian agent of the Government would take care of them, and instruct them in the art of tilling the ground, and raising abundant food, of weaving their cloathes, and manufacturing their tools; he intimated to one of them that the United States would probably treat with his nation for the cession of a strip of land for a road; and he promised to the other that they should return on iron horses, much swifter than any living horse could carry them.

After all, the Indians seemed pretty well comforted by receiving silver medals, and a large star-spangled flag. As the squaws were unexpected visitors, Mrs. Fillmore had nothing to give them but sugar-plums.

II. SITE OF THE CITY—POLITICS.

Washington is an artificial city, without any other importance than that it is the seat of the Government and of the Legislature of the United States. Like Munich, Stuttgart, or Karlsruhe,—expansions of the court of the Princes, built only by their command and encouragement, and therefore without importance for commercial intercourse,—Washington, too, has its origin, not in the natural requirements of the country, but in the decision of Congress, which

placed the seat of the government on the banks of
the Potomac. The riots in Philadelphia, when the
mutinous soldiers had threatened the Continental
Congress in Independence Hall, were a warning to
the statesmen of America not to put their government within the reach of the excitable population of
large cities. In order to prevent a pressure from
without, as dangerous for the dignity of the government as to the liberty of the people, it has become a
political maxim in every State to fix the Capitol* in
some central place, but not in the commercial metropolis. Boston is the only exception to this rule, but
the natural coolness of the New-Englanders divests
the experiment, of connecting the centre of commerce
with the seat of government, of the danger which
would encompass it in the excitable Middle States or
the South.

Though Washington was intended to be only a city
of the Government and of the Congress, yet there
was a secret hope that the vitality of the United
States might give an independent and growing life,
even to this artificial offspring. And why not? The
Potomac is a noble stream, which can carry steamers
and merchant-vessels as well as shads, and Chesapeak
Bay, into which it discharges its waters, has raised
Baltimore to prosperity. The city, therefore, was laid
out on a wide plan, but the great extension is not

---

* The statehouses of the States and the palace of the Congress
in Washington bear all this name.

yet filled up: the resources of the back country of Washington remained undeveloped, and therefore commerce does not impart life to the city; it has remained what it was in the beginning, the seat of the departments and officials. It spreads only in proportion as the extension of the territory of the United States leads to a natural increase of the members of Congress, of the government officers, and government expenditure. Washington is the best evidence that no city can grow up artificially where a government has no revenues to squander. Everything has here turned out differently from what had been intended. It strips bare the fact, that when a great city seems to be enriched at the will of a despot, this is only because the public revenues are artificially squandered on it, but no new wealth is created.

When the Capitol was laid out on the hill, the city was to grow up in front of the building, in the shape of a fan, and the White House, the residence of the President, to remain a country seat, at a distance of two or three miles from the city, that the President might not be importuned by frequent visitors. The grounds in front of the Capitol naturally rose in price, whilst the lots in the valley, sloping towards the White House, had no pretension of becoming the American metropolis, and remained cheap. But pre-cisely because they were cheap, they were taken up; buildings rose here and there very irregularly; and

when the central building was finished, it had nothing
but the fields in front, and it turned its back to the
city, of which the White House and the Capitol became
the two extremities. A dozen of columns were
thereupon patched to the back of the Congress-hall,
that it might become the front. Staircases were
made, and gardens laid out, to ornament the hill on
which it is raised; but all these changes have not
improved its style. From afar it looks commanding,
but as you approach and can distinguish the decorations, you see the meagreness of the design and the
meanness of the execution. In the old front it looks
better.

The general aspect of the city is very strange. The
Capitol, the Post Office, the Treasury, the Home
Office, the Smithsonian Institution, and the White
House, decorated with a profusion of white marble,
of dark granite, and architectural ornaments, form a
remarkable contrast to the unconnected patches of
low brick-houses which line the streets. These also
are broad enough for the traffic of a ten times larger
population than it is now. The American applies
proudly to his Capitol the lines of Horace : " Privatus
illus census erat brevis, commune magnum;" but to
a foreigner it makes the impression of an Eastern
metropolis of a half-nomade nation, where the palaces
of the king are surrounded by the temporary buildings of a people, held together only by the presence
of the court. And this is really the character of the

population of Washington. Society is formed here
by two distinct classes of inhabitants, one temporary,
the other permanent. For the President, the Heads
of Department, the Senators, and Members of the
House, it is but a temporary abode, it is not their
home; they live almost all in hotels and lodgings,
not in their own house. They do not care for
domestic comforts, and therefore they do not ornament
their abodes; they look on them as the banker does
on his dark and dreary counting-house. They remain
strangers in Washington. Even those who live here
for ten years and longer do not feel at home. Henry
Clay lived and died in a hotel, and during his long
career connected with Washington city, Mrs. Clay
never visited him, though their marriage was always
a happy one. The permanent population in the city,
are the clerks in the departments, the judges of the
Supreme Court, the editors of the papers, a few merchants and bankers, and the foreign ambassadors,
who keep house here, and in social respect have an
importance far superior to any that they could occupy
in Philadelphia or New York. They are the hosts
who give elegant dinners, and balls, and evening
parties. The members of Congress, and their wives
and daughters are the guests, unable to return at
Washington the hospitality they receive,—a position,
which, for a clever diplomatist, is of no small avail.
To the floating population belong also the agents for
elections, for private claims, and for government
grants; "the lobby members," as they are called,

who, like the sharks around the vessels, ply around the senators, rushing at every job and government contract. For political intriguers, there is no richer gold field in the United States than Washington,— an arena, not only of political contests, but also of *" log-rolling," " pipe-laying,"* and *" wire-pulling."*

As to the wire-pullers, they are known all over the political world; and the philosopher, studying history, is astonished, how men often act the part of puppets, without their own knowledge. The greatest wire-puller is, of course, Russian diplomacy; and the words legitimacy, demagogy, democracy, socialism, and family, are those by which European nations and statesmen are moved to dance as St. Petersburgh fiddles. In America, the magic word is different, it is called " peculiar institution," and " abolitionism." Whenever an opportunity is wanted to disturb men's minds, to raise politicians to greatness, or to bury others, the stage is always ready, and the play always successful. The plot is " secession from the Union," and the finale, " the country saved," with triumphal arches, and nosegays, and garlands, for the saviours of the country. Minor plays are daily enacted by the wire-pullers, who have a continual practice in the elections; where it is not only important to canvass for the friend, but also to weaken the enemy, by drawing off his votes for a third person.

" Log-rolling " is a more simple affair. It is the combination of different interests on the principle, " daub me and I daub thee." Whoever is too feeble to carry his own project, combines with others in the same position, in order to get influence. Local affairs and grants are often brought to notice and pass the Congress in this way.

Of " pipe-laying " I got two different definitions. According to one, the origin of this expression is traced to an election job, where an undertaker sold some Irish and German votes by a written agreement, in which, of course, the ware could not be named ; it was therefore styled *pipes* ; pipe-laying would therefore mean corruption. But it also applied to political manœuvres for an aim entirely different from what it seems to be. For instance, wishing to defeat the grant of land for a special railway or canal, which has every chance to pass, you vote for it, but in your speech you describe, in glowing colours, the advantages of railroads in general, and wind up, by presenting an amendment, for the extension of the grant to all the other railroads in construction,—on the principle of equality ; and thus you make the grant impossible.

In a democratic country, where freedom of speech is not limited, and the press is unfettered even by fiscal laws, every movement of government is exposed, judged, and condemned in the most unmeasured words. One party denounces the other, and corruption is mentioned so often, that it would be very easy for a malicious tourist to write a book on the decline of the United States, composed exclusively from extracts from public speeches, and party papers. But every impartial observer will find, that government is carried on in America with remarkable integrity and economy. Large as the Union is, the expenditure of the federal government, including the interest of the United States debt, and the annual payment towards its extinction, is met by the income from the duties on importation, and the sales of land. No direct taxes are levied for federal purposes. If we compare the estimates of the United States with the European budgets, we find that the sums expended without necessity, are much smaller than anywhere else, though the party criminations and recriminations are so loud, that a foreigner is tempted to believe the government to be a compound of corruption and dishonesty. The Galphin and Gardiner claims were often mentioned by the opposition as evidences of mismanagement. But they have been thoroughly investigated, and no blame could be attached to the departments. The Galphin claim arose out of old English pretensions from the Cherokee war. After many years' solicitation, it was fully established by Congress, and the attorney-general had no objection to it; but when it was paid, it appeared, that the acting secretary at war had formerly been the legal counsel of the claimant, and was entitled, in case of success, to a considerable share of the amount received. Though the justice of the claim was not disputed, the house blamed the President for not immediately dismissing the secretary at war; and a law was passed, prohibiting any senator,

member of the house, head of department, or any
public officer whosoever, to participate in any emolu-
ment proceeding out of claims before Congress.—
The Gardiner claim was paid under the treaty with
Mexico at Guadaloupe Hidalgo, where two million
dollars had been set aside for the discharge of all
claims of American citizens against the Mexican
government. This claim too was acknowledged by
Congress, and paid by the Treasury; yet it turned
out to be altogether a forgery. A committee was
appointed to inquire into the facts of the case, but
until now it has not found any connection of the
claimant with the departments of state. The secretary
of treasury had been originally the counsel of the
claimant, but had given up his interest in the cause,
as soon as promoted to office.

The Senate of the United States, as a body, contains more practical statesmanship and administrative
experience, than any other legislative assembly. All
its members have been trained in the legislative
assemblies and senates of the individual States.
Many of them have passed several years in the House
at Washington, or have been at the head of their
State as Governors, or have transacted the business
of the Union as Heads of the Departments of State.
But southern rashness sometimes deprives the Senate
of the gravity and dignity which behoves the fathers
of the great Republic.

During the session of 1852, Mr. Rhett, of South
Carolina, having, in a speech, violently and personally

attacked Mr. Clemens, of Alabama, was openly chal-
lenged by his opponent, in a reply more violent than
the attack. The Senator of South Carolina, however,
is not only chivalrous, but also pious; he declared to
the Senate, that he is a member of the church, and
that religion forbade him to fight, though, as it seems,
it had not restrained him from an abusive attack.—
But Solon Borland, the Senator of Arkansas, went
much farther, and rehearsed, with modern improvements, the scene of the Spartan chief, who, in the
council of war before the battle of Salamis, impatiently
raised his cane, when he saw that Themistocles was
about to speak. " Strike, but listen!" was the celebrated answer of the great Athenian, which disarmed
the angry Spartan. At the Capitol a similar scene
terminated differently. The estimates for printing
the last census seemed extravagant to the economical
Senator from the Red River; he could not conceive,
how the publication of the statistical details could be
of a use commensurate to the costs of printing, and
when Mr. Kennedy, the chief of the census office, in
order to explain the importance of the documents,
came to the seat of the Senator, and requested him
to listen to his explanation, the modern Solon of
Arkansas improved the part of the Spartan chief;
he raised his fist, knocked down Mr. Kennedy with a
powerful blow, and did *not* listen.

The House of Representatives, renewed every two
years, by general election, has here a more subordinate position, than in any other constitutional

realm. The great parliamentary battles are all fought
in the Senate. The speeches of the great American
orators, Clay, Webster, Calhoun, and Cass, have re-
sounded within its walls, and the eloquence of Soulé,
Seward, and Sumner, is equal to that of their illustrious
predecessors. Personal collisions, rare in the Senate,
are frequent in the House. During the last session
Messrs. Wilcox and Brown, both from Mississippi,
boxed one another's ears in open session. The
Tennesseean representative gave the lie to his col-
league from Kentucky, and abusive language was
often heard, though it was not a time of great political excitement, and no important question stirred up
the passions.

The powers of Congress are very different from
those of the legislative assemblies in other countries.
Congress does not govern, nor control the government
of the States; nor has it anything to do with the
Church, the Education, the Prisons, the civil or
criminal Law, or with private bills. The chief objects
of the English Parliament are, therefore, removed
from its sphere. Congress has only the power to
decide upon the commercial policy of the United
States, and to provide for their defence, and for certain
matters of general interest. It makes the tariff,
regulates commerce with foreign nations, coins money,
regulates its value, and provides for the punishment
of forgery. It fixes the standard of weights and
measures, establishes post-offices and post-roads,
defines and punishes piracy, and offences against the

law of nations. It declares war, raises and supports
armies, provides and maintains a navy, calls forth the
militia to execute the laws of the Union, and makes
rules for the regulation and government of the land
and naval forces. It borrows money on the credit of
the United States, votes the budget, and settles
claims against the federal government; it admits new
States, it exercises exclusive legislation in the district
of Columbia, and makes all needful regulations respecting any "Territory," or other property belonging
to the United States.   It has, moreover, to establish
a uniform rule of naturalisation, and uniform laws on
the subject of bankruptcies throughout the United
States.   The Senate has to discuss the treaties and
nominations of Ambassadors, and of the Judges of
the Supreme Court, made by the President, and to
try all impeachments of public officers. The Ministers, or, as they are called, the Heads of the Executive Departments, are not members of Congress, they
are only the advisers of the President, and it is not
necessary that they should have a parliamentary
majority. The chief function of European parlia-
ments, the defeat or support of the ministry, is,
therefore, not to be found at the Capitol. A Frenchman would find the Congress very dull, but, as a
President is elected every fourth year, by universal
suffrage, the American can easily spare the excitement of a ministerial crisis, though this is the
necessary safety-valve to constitutional Europe.

With such restricted powers—all those not men-

tioned in the Constitution as belonging to Congress
being reserved to the individual States—the members
of Congress and the Senators are not overwhelmed
by business. Unless, therefore, the Union needs
again to be saved from secession, or the tariff is discussed, or the admission of a new State, connected
with the question of slavery, to be decided—the spare
time of Congress is employed for personal explana-
tions, and political speeches, as they are called, or
"speeches for Buncombe," as they are nicknamed.
In fact, they are lectures on every topic which has
political interest, on slavery or abolition, on the land
system,. the Maine liquor-law, on the merits or
demerits of the parties, or on any other abstract
political principle, intended for the constituents of
the Representative or Senator, not for the House or
the Senate. This is so well understood, that members
often are considerate enough to announce, that they
will send their speeches straight to the congressional
newspaper, without robbing the House or Senate of
its time, by delivering them. But the great object
of Congress, every fourth year, is the making of a
President. The election belongs, of course, to the
people, but the masses are influenced from Washington; and therefore speeches on the merits of the
party nominees, and the defence of them against
party attacks, are great themes in the halls of the
Capitol. The session preceding the Presidential
election always lasts long, from the first Monday of
December often till the end of July. Then follows

a short one, closed after the inauguration of the new
President, which takes place on the 4th of March.
The ensuing session is again long and important,
succeeded by a short one; thus their duration alter-
nates from four to seven months.

III. KOSSUTH AND THE CONGRESS.—BANQUETS.—THE MONUMENTS OF WASHINGTON CITY.

The reception of Kossuth in New York, as a tribute
to the principles of freedom, had become a great
political event through the enthusiasm roused by his
speeches, in which he pointed out the interests and
obligations of America, in respect to foreign affairs.
He preached the principles of Christianity as extended
to international relations, and since he had undoubtedly touched the hearts of the people, a certain
political clique became frightened, and pains were
taken to arrest his triumphal progress, and to damp
the fire kindled by his eloquence. At the receipt of
the tidings about the French usurpation, the New
York Herald, and other papers began immediately to
say, that New York is excitable and easily carried
away by sudden emotions, but that Philadelphia will
prove cooler, and the enthusiasm subside step by step.
The corporation dinner at Philadelphia, was to be a
breakwater for the tide of popular excitement, and it
was arranged that the toasts should all be responded
to in the most complimentary way for " the nation's
guest," but disclaiming his explanation of the princi-

ples of non-intervention. As Kossuth was exhausted by his previous exertions, he could not make a speech at the dinner, and had soon to retire. At the same time Judge Kane and Judge Kelley defeated the scheme, by advocating, in eloquent words, the views and principles which had been applauded by the masses in New York. A second entertainment, called "the People's banquet," was arranged for the next day, and popular feeling burst forth in the Quaker city, not only for Kossuth, but also for his principles, and Baltimore responded yet more loudly to his appeal.

The Congress, always ready to follow the impulse of the people, hereupon invited him to the Capitol, an honour never before bestowed on anybody but Lafayette. A few southern members (six in number) delayed the decision for a couple of days by endless speeches and amendments; but they could not succeed in enlisting any more votes to this opposition.

On the 7th of January, the galleries and the lobbies in the Senate and the House, were overcrowded by ladies. Kossuth was introduced, the members rose from their seats, and Mr. Cartter, of Ohio, the chairman of the committee, said, " Mr. Speaker, I have the honour on the part of the committee, to present Governor Louis Kossuth to the House of Representatives."

The speaker responded, "As the organ of this body, I have the honour to extend to Louis Kossuth a cordial welcome to the House of Representatives." And Kossuth replied,

" Sir,—It is a remarkable fact in the history of mankind, that while through all the past honours were
bestowed upon glory, and glory was attached only to
success, the legislative authorities of this great Republic bestow honours upon a persecuted exile, not
conspicuous by glory, not favoured by success, but
engaged in a just cause. There is a triumph of
republican principles in this fact. Sir, I thank, in my
own and my country's name, the House of Representatives of the United States for the honour of this
cordial welcome."

He then took the seat which had been prepared for
him by the committee ; a motion was made to adjourn,
in order to afford the members an opportunity to pay
their respects to the guest of the Congress. The
members of the house, and the ladies advanced to the
circular area in front of the speaker's seat, and the
introductions recommenced once more.

In the evening of the same day a banquet was given
by the members of Congress, in honour of Kossuth.
The President of the Senate, Mr. King, of Alabama,
was in the chair. Mr. Lynn Boyd, the speaker of the
house, and Daniel Webster, the secretary of state,
occupied the places at the side of the " guest of the
nation ; " the majority of the senators and of the
ministers were present. Kossuth's speech was one of
his finest oratorical efforts, and some allusions to
American history and American statesmen called
forth a burst of enthusiasm such as I never had

witnessed before. The members rushed from their seats and pressed around the platform, and clapped their hands and gave such hearty cheers, that it was impossible to be mistaken as to the immense effect of the orator upon the minds of the audience. After him the Secretary of State delivered one of those emphatic speeches, in favour of struggling liberty—a homage and encouragement to those who had been defeated—which called back to remembrance his celebrated discourse for the Greeks. Another candidate for the Presidency followed him, Douglas of Illinois, and put his approbation of Kossuth's principles, as applied to American policy, in still more precise terms. General Cass went again a step further in his eloquent response to the next toast. General Houston, also a candidate for Presidency, saw that he could not safely do more, and therefore silently retired. His friends, alarmed by the success of the other candidates, called for him, but he was not to be found. The party separated in high spirits.

The next day was the anniversary of the battle of New Orleans, one of the great holidays of the democratic party. The Whigs were opposed to the war of 1812, and the hero of New Orleans, the obstinate democratic Jackson, is, of course, not in great favour with them : the celebration of the 8th of January has, therefore, always a party colour. A strong feeling against England often manifests itself on this occasion, especially since the emigration from Ireland has given some political power to the Celtic blood.

A certain section of the English people is very much mistaken in their estimate of the feelings of goodwill towards them across the Atlantic. They are a cool and calculating people, and seeing their commercial interests interwoven with those of the States so tightly, that they cannot be severed without a fatal injury to the financial prosperity of both countries, they listen with pleasure to their occasional guests from the American commercial States, who, in their after dinner speeches, so emphatically announce the good news of an everlasting friendship between the great Republic and the mighty constitutional Monarchy. The English of the Manchester school too easily forget, that nations are ruled not only by the gospel of Bentham and the revelations of Adam Smith, but also by other passions, by sympathies and antipathies not less powerful in their results than the love of lucre. Antipathy against England is deeply rooted in the heart of the Americans. Planted by religious communities,—Puritans, Roman Catholics, Quakers,—who had to leave their home in order to escape the oppression of an intolerant church, the colonies were forced into a long protracted war, by the encroachments of the central government. The barbarous Indians, on the frontiers, were incited against the peaceful settlers of the West; the expansion of the States west of the Southern Alleghanies, was interfered with by diplomatic intrigues; a new war proved necessary against England for the protection of American commerce and of the American

sailors, and wherever there rose an enemy of the
States, it was always a friend of England. The
Americans have not forgotten that their Capitol, the
sanctuary of the nation, the symbol of the Union,
was burnt down by English troops wantonly, as if it
were the Bala Hissar, at Kabul; and the "exodus"
which has relieved Ireland, and the poor-houses of
England, of hundreds of thousands,—a matter of
congratulation on this side of the Atlantic,—has
fanned the embers of animosity not yet extinguished
in the United States. Englishmen rarely notice
what an amount of hatred against their country is
exported by the emigrant ships, to be sown into a
fertile soil, where it easily ripens. The Irish emigrants, aroused from the torpor of their bogs, exert
their physical and intellectual power successfully on
the virgin settlements of the West, and when five
years have made them citizens of the United States,
their hearts are still filled with enmity against a
country, whose institutions have driven them from
their old home. The German emigrants, too, who
flee from the nameless oppression of their petty
tyrants, feel no sympathy for England. They say,
that England has always sided with their despotic
princes, and spent for their restoration hundreds of
millions sterling, whilst struggling liberty on the
continent has never received anything from the
English but some fine parliamentary speeches of
compassion. The manufacturer and the mechanic, who
have to compete with English imports, complain that

he is ruined by them; the slave-holder grumbles against the English nation on account of the Abolitionist feeling, and the "West Indian experiment." The anniversary of the battle of New Orleans is an opportunity suited for the utterance of such feelings; and this year it was Senator Stephen Douglas, of Illinois, who was the exponent of this tendency. Douglas, a short man with an uncommonly intelligent physiognomy, scarcely above forty years old, who, from being apprenticed to a cabinet maker, has become one of the leaders of the democratic party, is a most popular orator. Aware of the feelings of the masses, he has always the courage to express them without restraint. Deeply initiated in the secret machinery of the elections and political manœuvres, his influence in Congress and in the party conventions is not less powerful than in popular meetings. Most amiable in the intimacy of private life, he is, in public, the relentless enemy of his enemies, and the unconditional advocate of his political friends,—in every respect one of the important men of the Union.

Kossuth could not leave the hostile feeling against England unnoticed. He strongly dwelt on the fact, that a mutual, sincere friendship between America and England, is the only hope of the ultimate triumph of liberty all over the world. He expressed openly, that no better service ever can be done to the despots, than to throw the apple of discord between these two nations, and to foster a hostility, which, having its root in past wrongs, does not appertain to the present

condition of both states. He had often to repeat these
remarks during his progress in the United States.

The most interesting man in the Hall for me was
General Houston, of Texas. I had the opportunity
of meeting him several times during our stay in Washington, and was always struck by his un-American
manners. Reserved as an Indian, and polite as a
Spaniard, with a countenance alike impassable when
flattered by his admirers, and when assailed by his
opponents, he made upon me the impression of a great
man. People seemed surprised at my admiration for
" Sam Houston," but a man who, in the most different situations, had always reached the highest
position in the community where he lived, cannot be
of ordinary gifts. His ancestors were Scotch High-
landers, he himself a Virginian, but after the death of
his father, at the beginning of this century, his
mother removed to the western frontier of Tennessee,
close to the Indian boundary, in order to better her
broken fortunes. The schools of Virginia were never
much renowned, and Houston did not visit them frequently. In western Tennessee there were no schools;
he was placed in a merchant's store, and had to stand
behind the counter. But this did not suit his temper;
he escaped, and went to the Indians, where he lived
for several years, hunting the deer, and reading Daniel
de Foe, and Pope's Iliad. When eighteen, he returned
to his home, and became a teacher; then enlisted
in the U.S. army, at the time of the war with England.
He was wounded at the battle of the Horse-shoe,

against the Creeks, on the Tallapoosa river, and got a
Lieutenancy as a reward for his toils and bravery. But
after the peace, he threw off his commission, studied
law, put up his shingle,* and in the course of a few
years was elected District Attorney, in Tennessee,
Militia General, Member of Congress, and in 1827,
Governor of the State. He married, but being unhappy in marriage, and assailed by the calumnies of
the friends of his wife, he resigned his office as
Governor, left civilized society, and went again into
the Indian wilderness, to live amongst his early friends
the Cherokees.

Intimate with their king, he soon became the coun-
sellor of the nation. They felt towards him the
affection of old and tried friends. He knew their
wrongs, and was resolved to scrutinize the actions of
the Indian agents and sub-agents. His feelings we
may gather from one of his later speeches :—

" During the period of my residence among the
Indians, in the Arkanses region, I had every facility
of gaining a complete knowledge of the flagrant outrages practised upon the poor red men by the agents of
the government. I saw, every year, vast sums squandered and consumed without the Indians deriving the
least benefit, and the government in very many instances utterly ignorant of the wrongs that were
perpetrated. Had one-third of the money advanced
by the government been usefully, honourably, and
wisely applied, all those tribes might have been now

---

* Americanism; it means to begin business as lawyer.

in possession of the arts and the enjoyments of civilisation. I care not what dreamers, and politicians,
and travellers, and writers say to the contrary. I
know the Indian character, and I confidently avow,
that if one-third of the many millions of dollars our
government has appropriated within the last twenty-
five years, for the benefit of the Indian population,
had been honestly and judiciously applied, there would
not have been at this time a single tribe within the
limits of our states and territories, but what would
have been in the complete enjoyment of all the arts
and all the comforts of civilised life. But there is not
a tribe but has been outraged and defrauded, and
nearly all the wars we have prosecuted against the
Indians, have grown out of the bold frauds and the
cruel injustice played off upon them by our Indian
agents and their accomplices."

Personally acquainted with President Jackson,
Houston visited Washington in 1832, to plead the
cause of the red men. But the friends of those
whom he had denounced were powerful; and though
he succeeded in his object, as far as the Indians
were concerned, he was assailed personally in the
most violent way, until he horsewhipped in the open
street one of his enemies, a member of Congress.
He was tried, but his defence was so able, that he
was only sentenced to be reprimanded by the Speaker
at the bar of the House. In the mean time, difficulties had arisen between the Mexican province,
Texas, and the central government of Mexico.

Houston, known as an enterprising man, was invited to settle in the new State, which had need of
bold soldiers.   But even here people found great
fault with him; he had adopted the Indian dress,
the buckskin breeches, and the Mexican blanket.
When, however, the war broke out, sinews and brains
rose in demand; and, in spite of the Indian dress,
Houston was elected commander-in-chief of "the
patriots."   In those lonely countries, where it is
difficult to find provisions, the armies of the contending parties are not so numerous as in Europe.
The Texan general mustered 700 men on the field
of San Jacinto (21st April, 1836); Santa Anna, the
Mexican President, who commanded in person, had
1800.   The battle was fought gallantly, the American
riflemen did their work with the skill of experienced
hunters, and in the evening the Mexican army was
annihilated, and their commander-in-chief a prisoner
of war.   The Independence of Texas was won.   But
a greater task was to be achieved; the new Republic
was to be organised, and the elements of society were
here very strange.   Spaniards, American pioneers,
hunters, adventurers, and outlaws, a band not dis-
similar to the founders of Rome, and to the followers
of Rollo of Normandy, or of William the Conqueror,
formed the nucleus of the first population of the
" Lone Star Republic."   Houston was the only man
there who, with an army of such men, could achieve
the independence of a State, and organise the country
from the chaos.   The government had nothing but

debts; they had neither money nor credit. But Houston knew how to treat the people with whom he had conquered the enemy. An American gentleman, at this time accidentally a resident of Texas, told me, that when the masses pressed upon the general to become a candidate for the Presidency of Texas, and requested him to address them, he went on the platform, and with a glance of contempt, he said—" Gentlemen, do you know what I feel when I see you claiming a government? Nothing but disdain and disgust. Here I see amongst you the adventurer, the bankrupt, the swindler, the gambler, the outlaw, the murderer from all the States of the Union—men able to fight and to defeat all the armies of the world; but as to the organisation of a government, which should secure peace, prosperity, and power at home, and command the respect of civilised nations — Gentleman, this is not your task. Nothing but an iron hand can rule you; and, if you elect me, by the Almighty, you shall have it!" " Hurrah for old Sam!" was the response, and on the 22d of October, Sam. Houston was inaugurated the first President of Texas. With what ability he managed, first the recognition of independence by foreign nations, then the annexation to the United States, and at last an indemnity of ten millions of dollars, for the land which was ceded by Texas to the federal government at the establishment of the Territory of New Mexico, is but another evidence of the powers of the man; who, nevertheless, as he is not a great debater, seems not to command much personal influence in the Senate of Washington. To me, he is the representative of a new class of statesmen, who, developed in the western wilderness, will probably in a short time succeed to the present refined school of eloquent lawyers and politicians in the management of the great Republic. It is almost unnecessary to remark that the society of Texas has entirely altered since the times of the battle of San Jacinto, and that it partakes now of the character of the South and of the West.

There can scarcely be a greater contrast than between the reserved warrior, who has wrested a great State from Mexico, and has annexed it to the United States, in spite of the opposition of both Republics, and of all the intrigues of European diplomacy—and the young and eloquent "Free-soil" Senator of Massachusetts, Charles Sumner. The one, educated by nature amongst the Indians—the other the refined student, reared in the schools of New England, and maturing his learning in Europe amongst German professors, and English statesmen. The one, extending the frontiers of his country in a southern direction, and therefore adding new territory to slavery; the other, bent on the purpose of restraining the "peculiar institution," and an advocate of the principles of freedom extended to the Black. The one, accustomed to war; the other, a disciple of the "Peace Society;" the one the practical, the other the theoretical friend of the red man. Charles Sumner had for the first time entered the

Senate this session. He occupies there a strange
position; he does not belong to either of the two
great parties, he is a Free Democrat, without any
other political co-religionist than Hale of Maine, and
Chase of Ohio. But he does not care for momentary
success; he stands and falls with the principles he
advocates, disclaiming a compromise.

Pierre Soulé, of Louisiana, is the most brilliant
orator of the Senate. A Frenchman by birth, he
unites the advantages of European education with
the republican experience of America. He under-
stands the importance of the department of foreign
affairs, and does not indulge in the national vanity,
that America, though connected by commerce with
the whole world, should maintain that political isolation which once was necessary for the growing State.
He knows that the time has come, when the great
Commonwealth has to take a seat in the council of
nations, and to throw her weight in the scale in
which the destinies of nations are weighed. He is
an ornament of the Democratic party.

Amongst the members of the house none interested
me so much as Horace Mann, from Massachusetts,—
the mild and simple-hearted statesman, the advocate
of the oppressed, the great reformer of the schools of
Massachusetts. His merits are less ostentatious than
those of others of his colleagues, but his influence is
as lasting as the universal esteem for the purity of
his character. The present school-system of his
State is his monument.

The Navy-yard at Washington, though smaller in
size than similar establishments in England or France,
is remarkable for the improvements of the machines
for the fabrication of arms and ammunition. The
bullets are cut here, not cast; the testing of the
brass for guns was novel to me; I saw some improvements on the locks of the cannons, and on their
carriages; and a new method for the construction of
shells, which enables one to determine the distance
at which they are to burst. The liberality of the
government allowed us not only to see, but also to
examine all the details of the construction, which, in
Europe, are jealously guarded like secrets of state.

The Patent office is a kind of historical museum
and exhibition of American industry. Samples of
all the improvements and inventions, which have been
patented by the United States, show the progress of
the inventive genius in America. A series of the
tools, weapons, clothing, and embroidery of the Indian
tribes, are specimens of native industry; an ethno-
logical collection from the South Sea, stuffed American
animals, specimens of coal and ore, offer an interesting source of instruction, though the museum is far
from complete. But the readiness and kindness with
which the gentlemen superintending the office give
every explanation, and especially all the statistical
details about the manufactures and agriculture of the
United States, afford an insight into the present condition and capability of the fabrication, and the
increasing production of the Union.

APPENDIX.

THE Northmen were a people of princes and pirates. They left their country either to get a crown and to found an aristocracy in foreign realms, or to meet the ignominious death of piratical invaders. Rurik goes eastwards to be the prince of Russia and the founder of her aristocracy; the outlaw Rolf Gange (Rollo) wins Normandy in France by his sword; William the Bastard becomes the Conqueror; Robert Guiscard gets a kingdom in Naples, and Bohemund a dukedom in Antiochia.

Naddod, the Norwegian pirate, had discovered Iceland in the second half of the ninth century, and the snowy island soon became an asylum for oppressed freedom exiled from Norway. The king of the latter country was but the first amongst his equals down to the time when king Harold made proposals by messengers to a girl called Gyda, the daughter of a chief and the fosterchild of a freeman. We read that Gyda replied to the messengers : " Now tell to king Harold these my words—I will only agree to be his lawful wife upon condition that he shall first, for my sake, subject to himself the whole of Norway, so that he may rule over the kingdom as freely and fully as king

Erik over Sweden, or Gorm the Old over Denmark, for only then methinks can he be called the king of a people." King Harold became thoughtful, and made a solemn vow never to clip or comb his hair until he had subdued the whole of Norway, with scot, and duties, and domains, or if not, to die in the attempt.

Ten years later he had become sole king over all Norway, and he sent his men to the proud girl, and made her his lawful wife, and he went to a bath and had his hair dressed and cut, which had been uncut and uncombed for ten years: he had been called *Ugly Head*, but now he won the name Harfager, or Fair Hair.

Several of the chiefs and freemen, who would not submit to the despotic rule of the king, fled from Norway. Ingolf, one of them, and his followers went to Iceland, taking with him as his household gods the columns raised in front of his house. When he approached the shore of the new land which was to become his home, he cast them overboard, in order to ascertain where he had to fix his dwelling; for it was the custom to fix it wherever the door-posts were driven ashore : but they floated for a long time, and were driven out of sight. He landed therefore on a point unsanctioned by the omen; and when his servants had, three years later, found these very columns cast ashore at a great distance, he removed his family to the spot, though uninviting and sterile, and erected there his dwellings, and the place was called Reykiavik, and remains until now the capital of Iceland. The isle has been ever since an asylum for freedom and science. " New England perhaps and Iceland are the only modern colonies ever founded on principles, and peopled at first from higher motives than want or gain; and we see at this day a lingering spark in each of a higher mind than in populations which have set out from a lower level."*

A hundred years after Ingolf, Erik, surnamed the Red, fled to Iceland, having committed a homicide in Norway. But in Iceland too he got into quarrels with his neighbours, and having suffered an injury, rashly avenged it by the death of the offender. Condemned to banishment at Thornæsthing, he fitted out a vessel, determined to seek the country in the West, which a seafarer was said to have seen when driven by storm into the Western ocean. He soon found land, explored it, and called it Greenland, in order to induce other Icelanders to settle here, and returned for this purpose to Iceland (985). In the ensuing summer he returned to the land which he had discovered, to fix there his permanent residence, accompanied by many friends and adventurers, amongst whom Heriulf was one of the most prominent, the father of Biarni. Biarni was a youth of great promise, bold and adventurous, seized with an irresistible desire to travel, and by travelling successful in obtaining both fortune and honour. He passed his winters alternately abroad and at home with his father, and

* Sam. Laing, ' Seakings of Norway.'

had arrived in Iceland from a journey to Norway, just when his father had left the island. Biarni, informed of the departure of Heriulf, was unwilling to disembark, and when the sailors enquired what course he intended to pursue, he replied: "To do as I have been accustomed, and spend the winter with my father; I wish, therefore, to proceed to Greenland, if you are willing to accompany me thither."—They assented, and Biarni said, "Our course seems somewhat foolish, when none among us has ever crossed the Greenland ocean." Nevertheless, they put out to sea, when they had refitted their vessel. They made sail for three days, but strong north-easterly wind, accompanied by thick fogs, carried them they knew not whither. At length they saw land, but according to the description it could not be Greenland; it was not mountainous, but hilly and covered with wood. They left it to the larboard, and sailed two days before they saw land again, it was flat and covered with wood. Then again they stood out to sea, with a south-west wind, and saw a third land, high, and the mountains covered with glaciers, and coasting along it they saw it was an island. Biarni did not land, because the country seemed little inviting, but stood out to sea with the same south-west wind, and sailing with fresh gales, reached, in four days more, Heriulfsness, in Greenland, his father's abode, and remained there all the time his father lived.

After the death of Heriulf, Biarni visited Norway,

and was blamed, when he told of his discovery, for not
having examined the countries more accurately. But
Leif, the son of Erik the Red, who in the meantime
had also visited Norway, and had become there a
Christian, had in Iceland an interview with Biarni, and
bought of him his ship, which he fitted out and
manned with thirty-five men, in the year 1000. Erik
was to become the leader of the expedition, urged
upon by Leif, with assurances that the good fortune
of the family would attend him, but when all was
ready, and Erik was riding down on horseback to the
vessel, which lay near to his residence, his horse
stumbled, and Erik said, "Fortune will not permit
me to discover more lands than this which we inhabit.
I will proceed no farther with you." Erik then re
turned home, and Leif went on board with his companions, among whom was a man from Germany
named Tyrker.

They set sail, and the first land to which they came
was that last seen by Biarni. They made for land,
cast anchor and put out a boat; but having landed
they found no herbage, frozen heights all above, and
the whole space between them and the sea was occupied by bare flat rocks, and Leif said, "We will not do
as Biarni did, who never set foot on shore; I will give a
name to this land, and will call it Helluland, the land
of broad stones." (Now the isle of Newfoundland.)

After this they put out to sea and came to another
land : they approached, and set foot ashore ; it was
low and level and covered with wood ; in many places

where they explored it, there were white sands, and a
gradual rise of the coast.   Then said Leif, " This land
shall take its name from that which most abounds
here, it shall be called Markland, the land of woods."
(Nova Scotia.)   They then re-embarked as quickly
as possible, and sailed for two days with a north-east
wind till they again came in sight of land, approaching
which they touched upon an island, lying opposite to
the north-easterly part of the coast.   Here they landed
and found the air remarkably pleasant.   They observed
the grass covered with much dew, when they touched
this accidentally and raised the hand to the mouth,
they perceived a sweetness which they had not noticed
before.   Returning to their ships they sailed through
a bay, lying between the island and a promontory
running towards the north coast, and directing their
course westward, they passed beyond this promontory.
In this bay, when the tide was low, there were shallows
left of very great extent.   So great was the desire of
the men to land, that, without waiting for the high
tide to carry them nearer, they went ashore at a place
where a river poured out of a lake.   With the tide
they passed first up the river and then into the lake.
Having cast anchor they disembarked, and erected
first temporary, and subsequently more permanent
dwellings, having determined to remain there during
the winter.   Both in the river and in the lake there
was a great abundance of salmon, and of greater size
than they had before seen.   So great was the goodness
of the land, that they conceived that cattle would be

able to find provender in winter, none of that intense cold occurring to which they were accustomed in Greenland and Iceland, and the grass not withering very much. The equality in the length of days was greater than in their country, and on the shortest day the sun rose and set at the same time that it rises and sets on the 17th of October at Skalholt in Iceland (from Eyktarstad to Dagmalastad).

Their dwellings being completed, Leif divided his men into two companies, to explore the country and guard the houses, on alternate days. It happened one evening that one of the company was missing, Tyrker, the German, who had lived with Leif and his father a long time, and had been very fond of Leif in his childhood. He was of great importance for the colony, because he was possessed of great skill in every kind of smiths' work. Leif severely blamed his comrades, and went himself with twelve others to seek the man: when they had gone but a short distance from the dwellings, Tyrker met them, to their great joy—he had found vines and grapes; he knew them because he was brought up in a land where there was abundance of vines and grapes. The joy of Leif must really have been great, for he had become a Christian in Norway, and Christianity beginning to spread in Greenland and Iceland, the wine, indispensable for the communion, was of the highest importance for those distant northern regions. They now gathered grapes and felled timber, to load their ships, and made all ready for their departure, and Leif called the land Vinland, the land of wine; by the description evidently a part of New England, Connecticut, Rhode Island, and Massachusetts.*

They then put out to sea, having a fair wind, and at length came within sight of Greenland and her icy mountains, where they farther saved the crew of Thorer, the Norwegian, who was wrecked on a rock in the sea,—and sailed with them to Eriksfiord, until they reached Brattahlid, the residence of Erik. This expedition contributed both to the wealth and honour of Leif, and from that time he was called Leif the Lucky.

During the next winter, Erik the Red died in his ancient faith, unwilling to abandon it in his old age. Imbued with pagan pride, he said that his son's luck and ill-luck balanced each other; for if Leif had

---

* The discovery of wines is the best evidence that Vinland could not lie farther north than Massachusetts; on the other side, several authors, unacquainted with America, inferred from the absence of the cultivation of vines in New England, that the Icelandic Sage is altogether mythical. It is singular in this respect, that all the first English expeditions to Massachusetts did mention the abundance of vines. Philip Amidas and Captain Barlow write in 1585, " They found their first landing-place very sandy and low, *but so full of grapes*, that the very surge of the sea overflowed them, of which they found such plenty in all places, both on the sand, the green soil, and hills, as in the plains; as well on every little shrub, as also climbing towards the tops of high cedars, *that they did think in the world were not like abundance*." Capt. Bar. Gosmoll in 1602 : " In the island is a lake near a mile in circuit, the rest overgrown with trees, which so well as the bushes were so *overgrown with vines*, we could scarcely pass them—which made us call the island *Marthe's Vineyard*. The relation of Capt. Edward Haslow in 1614, in the description of Massachusetts, mentions the alkermes, currants, mulberries, *vines*, and gooseberries, as indigenous fruits.

found Vinland the Good, and saved a wreck in the ocean, he had brought also a hurtful person with him to Greenland, and that was the priest.

Leif succeeded his father as chieftain in Greenland, and could not easily leave that country again, but he felt all the importance of the discovery of the great Western mainland. Timber was an article of first necessity for the woodless northern regions, colonised by bold seafarers, and the grapes a luxury too much coveted. Leif therefore sent an expedition, under the command of his brother Thorwald, in the following spring to Vinland. They arrived safely at Leifsbudir,—the dwellings erected by Leif—and remained there for two years, supporting themselves by catching fish, and exploring the country in different directions, in the interior, and along the shore. But here, for the first time, they met natives, and killed nine of them; the others escaped to their canoes, and returning next morning with their friends assailed the Northmen. Thorwald was wounded by a poisoned arrow, and died. His companions buried him at a place which he had found previously so pleasant, that he wished to fix his habitation there; and they put a cross at his head and another at his feet, and called the place Krossa-Ness, the promontory of crosses. In the following spring (1005), they returned to Greenland, and conveyed the melancholy intelligence to Leif.

Hearing the account of his brother's death, Thorstein, the third son of Erik, was seized with a strong

desire to pass over to Vinland, to fetch the body of
his brother Thorwald, and to bury it in a consecrated
ground.   He fitted out a vessel and manned it with
twenty-five men, selected for their strength and stature, besides himself and Gudrid his wife, whom he
had married shortly before. Gudrid, according to the
Icelandic account of the discovery of America, excelled
all other women in beauty and in every accomplishment and grace, and she knew that she was destined
to an uncommon fate. Thorbiorn, her father, had
lived in Iceland in a liberal and sumptuous way,
regardless of his income.   He delighted in magnificence and entertained his friends in a princely
manner.   Once he gave a great feast in spring : the
company was numerous, and the banquet splendid,
and he said to his guests : " I have lived here long
and have found all men kind and friendly, and all our
intercourse has been most happy. At length, however, I find myself threatened with pecuniary difficulties, although till this time I have been considered to
abound in wealth.   I prefer to leave the country
rather than lose the station which I hold ; wherefore
I design to seek a home elsewhere, in preference to
reducing my present establishment. I shall rely on
the promises which Erik the Red, my friend, made
when we separated. I have determined in the ensuing
summer to go to Greenland." All were grieved at
this sudden change, for Thorbiorn was much beloved;
they knew however that it was in vain to expostulate.

Thorbiorn presented gifts to all; the banquet closed,

and each returned to his own home. He sold his lands, and bought a ship, and put out to sea, and many of his friends accompanied him. But the passage was unlucky, they met with many disasters. Disease attacked them, half of the whole company died, and all the survivors underwent much suffering and hardship. It was but in the beginning of winter that they reached Heriulfsness, in Greenland, where Thorkel, a man of great authority, extended his hospitality to them, though there was at that time a great scarcity in Greenland, for those who had gone out, had some of them returned with small supplies, others had not returned at all.

Thorkel was anxious to ascertain when the present scarcity would be relieved; he therefore invited a fortune-teller, Thorbiong, called the Little Witch, the only survivor of nine sisters, all fortune-tellers.

An elevated seat was prepared for her, on which was a cushion, stuffed with cocks' feathers. When evening was come, the witch arrived. Her outer garment was a blue cloak, trimmed all over with ribands, and ornamented with precious stones all round the border. She had on a necklace with glass beads; on her head she wore a black hood, made of lamb's skin, lined with white cat's skin. She carried in her hand a staff adorned with copper and precious stones, fixed into its head. Her girdle was of bark, from which hung a large leather pouch; her high shoes, covered with hair, were of calf's skin, with long latchets, to the extremities of which were fastened little bells of tin; her gloves were of cat's skin, white, and hairy on the inside.

She was received with the utmost respect, and at the dinner she got a mess of goat's milk, and the hearts of all animals which could be obtained; she used a copper spoon and a brazen knife, with a handle of a twisted tooth, and the point of which was broken.

The next day, towards evening, all preparations were made which she required for her incantations. She desired that some women should be found who could sing the *Vardlokkur;* mystic verses, alluring the tulelary genii. But no women could be found able to sing those verses, when Gudrid said, "I am neither learned nor a prophetess, but Halldis, my friend, taught me a song in Iceland, which she called Vardlokkur, but I cannot take any part in this matter, for I am a Christian maid." The witch replied, —"You may render great assistance to others, and without any loss to yourself." Then Thorkel endeavoured to persuade Gudrid, until she consented to do as he wished. Then all the women surrounded the place of incantation, the witch sitting on an elevation in the midst, and Gudrid sang the mystic verses in tones so sweet, and with such grace, that each one present thought he had never heard anything so harmonious or sweet before.

The fortune-teller declared then to Thorkel, that the scarcity will not endure, the coming spring will hail a happier year, and the diseases which now oppress the people will leave them soon. Turning now to Gudrid: " To you," she said, " for the assistance which you have rendered, I will give an immediate reward, for your future is known to me. You will marry a man here in Greenland, of most honourable station; but you will not enjoy him long, for your life will be passed in Iceland, where a great and noble race shall spring from you. A more glorious destiny awaits your offspring than it is in my power to testify. And now, daughter, hail, and fare thee well."

The witch was yet entreated by several others, and her responses did not err, but Thorbiorn went away from a house where such superstitions were entertained. The weather became milder, and Thorbiorn proceeded to Brattahlid, where Erik received him friendly, and gave him land, and Thorbiorn built a sumptuous mansion, and soon after, his daughter Gudrid married Thorstein, the youngest son of Erik, and accompanied him in his pious enterprise of bringing back the corpse of Thorwald from Vinland to Greenland. But the expedition was ill fated; through the whole summer they were tossed on the deep, and driven they knew not whither. At last they made land, and found that they were at the west coast of Greenland, and met there Thorstein, the heathen, surnamed the Swarthy, with his wife Grimhild, lone settlers on the inhospitable shore. Thorstein, Erik's son, and Gudrid, proceeded to their house. The expedition had much to suffer during winter (1005-6), a severe disease attacked the sailors, and carried off many of them; but Thorstein would not leave them in unconsecrated ground, and had coffins made for all the bodies, for he intended to carry them all to Eriksfiord in the ensuing summer. One evening Grimhild went out with Gudrid, and when the ladies had reached the outer door, Grimhild uttered a loud cry. She had seen the whole band of the dead men moving along, and amongst them she had seen herself, and Thorstein, Erik's son, with a whip in his hand, lashing the crowd before him. When she came back into the house she fell ill, and before morning she died. At the close of the same day Thorstein, Erik's son, died also, and Gudrid, his wife, was much afflicted; but after midnight he rose once more, and told to Gudrid that those are blessed who hold the Christian faith, for they will have salvation and mercy; but many observe the faith but ill, and men are buried in unconsecrated ground, and few funeral rites are performed; therefore he wished, with the other dead men, to be buried in a consecrated church, and his money divided between the church and the poor. Having thus spoken he expired.

Thorstein the Swarthy did all that his guest had wished for, and in the following spring he sold his farm and cattle, and carried Gudrid and all her property down to Brattahlid, to Leif; and Gudrid had her husband and the others buried in the church, with proper funeral rites, and remained in the family of Leif.

In autumn, Thorfinn, surnamed Karlsefne (of manly endowment), an Icelander of kingly lineage, came with Biarni Grimolfson and Thorhall Gamlason, on a mercantile expedition, with three ships to Eriks-fiord, in Greenland. They remained the winter with Leif, and after Christmas, Thorfinn began to treat with him as to the marriage of Gudrid, Leif being the person to whom the right of betrothment belonged. The chief had no objection to make, and the nuptials were celebrated at Brattahlid during the same winter, and a new expedition was prepared to Vinland the Good, on a large scale, for the charms of a comparatively southern climate had an irresistible force upon the imagination of the Icelanders. Thorfinn, Biarni, and Thorhall made up their mind to visit the country with their ships, and Freydisa, the natural daughter of Erik, with her husband Thorward, went with them. There were a hundred and sixty men in all; they took with them all kinds of live stock, for they designed to colonise the land, and Leif granted to Thorfinn all the use of the dwellings he had erected in Vinland, but he did not give them to him.

They sailed first to the west coast of Greenland, then to the northern coast of the American Continent, Helluland Mikla, the land of vast flat stones and foxes (Labrador). They came then to Markland, covered with wood, in which were many wild animals (Nova Scotia); and at last to Vinland. There were two Scots on board, a man Haki, and a woman Hekia, given to Leif by King Olaf Trygwason in Norway, and Leif had given them to Thorfinn because they were swifter of foot than wild animals. Thorfinn put these Scots on shore, directing them to run over the country for three days and then return. The ships lay-to during their absence; when they returned, one carried in his hand a bunch of grapes, the other an ear of corn. Thorfinn knew now that he was near Vinland, and they continued their course along the shore until they came to a fiord, which penetrated far into the land, and they called it Stromfiord (probably Buzzard Bay). On the mouth of it there was an island with strong currents round it, and they found such a vast number of eyder ducks on the island, that they could scarcely walk without treading on the eggs. They directed their course into this bay, disembarked, and made preparations for remaining, for the situation of this place was pleasant, and they found abundance of pasturage for their cattle. In autumn a son was born to Thorfinn and Gudrid; they called him Snorri Thorfinnson, the first child of European blood born in the mainland of America, the ancestor of the most celebrated sculptor of our age, Thorwaldsen. This founder of the Museum of Copenhagen is the lineal descendant of Thorfinn and Gudrid.

At Stromfiord they passed the winter, but it was very severe; they could neither hunt nor fish, and their provisions ran short. They prayed to God that

he would send them food, but the prayer was not
answered so soon as they desired.   They were deceived
in their dreams about Vinland the Good, and their
feelings are very well expressed in the verses which
Thorhall sang when he was carrying water to his
ship :

> I left the shores of Eriksford
> To seek, oh cursed Vinland! thine,
> Each warrior pledging there his word
> That we should here quaff choicest wine.
> Great Odin, warrior god, see how
> These waterpails I carry now,
> No wine my lips have touched, but low
> At humblest fountain I must bow.

Thorhall, called the Hunter, had been always ill
affected to Christianity since its introduction in Iceland, and as he saw that the prayers of the others
had no success, he went on the top of a rock, and
mumbled out his incantations to his gods.   A short
time after, a whale was cast ashore, they dressed it,
and all ate of it, and Thorhall said : " Now you see
that Thor is more ready to give aid than your Christ.
This food is the reward of a hymn which I composed
to Thor, who has rarely forsaken me."   When they
heard this, none would eat any more ; and so they
threw all the remainder of the flesh from the rocks,
commending themselves to God.   After which the
air became milder, they were again able to go fishing
and hunting, and there was abundance of eggs taken
on the island, and of fish caught in the sea, and of
wild animals on the mainland.

In spring, Thorhall and his party separated from Thorfinn, and went north to explore Vinland; but they were met by an adverse tempest, and driven off on to the coast of Ireland, and there made slaves.

Thorfinn sailed towards the south-west, to Mount Hope Bay; they found wild corn where the land was low, and where it rose higher vines were found; every river was full of fish, and in the forest there were a great number of wild animals. They passed a month here carelessly before they found any natives; the first they saw seemed to be much astonished, and retired. Thorfinn and his companions erected dwellings at a little distance from the lake, and in the next spring they began to trade with the natives, who desired above all things to obtain some red cloth, in exchange for which they offered various kinds of skins,—the first beginning of the American fur trade. They were anxious also to purchase swords and spears, but this Thorfinn forbade; in the same way as afterwards it became a capital crime, at the time of the settlement of Virginia, to sell muskets to the Indians. of Powhattan's confederacy.

But Thorfinn's colony had soon after to contend with all the difficulties which so often disturbed the prosperity of the later settlers. The natives came on them with fearful howling, and Thorfinn's party, surprised by the sudden attack, began to flee along the course of the river. In vain did Freydisa, a woman of manly courage, who in the state of pregnancy could not keep up with them, try to rally them. She was pursued by the Indians, and as she saw a man lying dead, she seized his sword which lay naked by his side, and brandished it against the natives, who were seized by a panic and fled back to their canoes.

Thorfinn and his followers extolled the courage of Freydisa, they dressed their own wounds and buried their dead; but they thought it obvious, that although the quality of the land was excellent, yet there would always be danger to be apprehended from the natives; they therefore prepared to depart, and returned first to Stromfiord, and after a second encounter with the natives, to Markland and Greenland. They had been absent for three years, and brought back the most valuable cargo, but Biarni Grimolfson was driven out into the ocean, and nothing was ever heard of him. Thorfinn returned afterwards to Norway, where he was honoured by all the great men, and settled definitely in Iceland. From him and his wife sprang a numerous and illustrious race, and several of the first men in Denmark, up to the present day, trace their pedigree to him. After his death, Gudrid took a journey to Rome, and passed the remainder of her life in the solitude of a convent in Iceland.

In 1011, a ship from Norway came to Greenland; the vessel belonged to two brothers, Helge and Tinboge, who wintered in Greenland. And Freydisa proposed to them, to join in a new expedition to Vinland, each party to have thirty men, and to divide the gain equally. They agreed and set out, and

reached Leif's booths, where they spent the winter;
but Freydisa, who had taken five men more with her
than the agreement allowed, quarrelled with the
brothers; murdered them, with the whole of their
people, and returned in spring to Greenland. Her
conduct excited the anger of Leif, and he withheld
from her children all places of trust and honour.

———

I cannot leave this interesting chapter of the first
discovery of America, without mentioning one Icelandic Saga more, which needs but the rhythmic
form to be one of the most charming ballads; it is
the Saga of the minstrel Biorn Asbrandson Breid-
vikingakappi, the champion of Breidavick.

Thorbiorn the Fat had married the sister of the
champion, and after her death the beautiful Thurid.
He was killed in an affray, and Snorri Godi, the
brother of Thurid, undertook the process for the
death of Thorbiorn, and also obliged his sister to
remove to his own house, for it was rumoured that
Biorn Asbrandson paid close attention to her, and
Snorri deemed him not wealthy enough to be the
husband of his sister. He gave her away to Thorodd,
the rich merchant of Froda, but Biorn Asbrandson
paid her frequent visits at her own house at Froda,
and Thorodd was blamed by Orn and Val, the sons
of Thorer, that he suffered the visits of Biorn, and

sat in the house when the minstrel was talking to
Thurid. Thorodd, therefore, with his two friends,
and two of his men, were determined to kill Biorn,
who, warned by Thurid, bade her a mournful farewell, and went on his way homeward. As he was
mounting the hill Digramul, five men leaped out
upon him from ambush; the sons of Thorer pressed
him hard and wounded him, but he slew them both,
whilst Thorodd and his men fled. But Snorri Godi
instituted a process against Biorn, in the court of
Thornaesting, on account of the slaughter of the sons
of Thorer, and Biorn was exiled for three years, and
his father Abrand had to pay the usual fines.

Biorn went now to Jomsburg, in Pomerania, and
was admitted into the fellowship of the knights of
Jomsburg, a band of adventurous pirates, heathens
and enemies of the Christians, organised by Toko,
their chief, into a formidable company, courted and
attacked in turn by the Northern kings, according to
their interest. Biorn fought here many a bloody
battle, and was esteemed a man of extraordinary
courage. When Toko died, Biorn returned to Iceland, and was since always called the Champion of
Breidavik. He lived in great splendour and luxury,
in the manner of courtiers and nobles, and he was
highly esteemed, because he was active and vigilant,
and highly skilled in martial exercises.

Soon after the return of Biorn, a general market
was held on the Bay of Froda, and all the merchants

rode thither, clad in coloured garments, and there was a great assemblage. Thurid, of Froda, was also there, and Biorn immediately entered into conversation with her, and no one censured them for talking long together, for it had been several years since they had met. But Thorodd disliked this, and he bribed a witch, by a large sum, to raise a snow storm against Biorn, should he ever cross the hills to visit Thurid.

In winter Biorn went to Froda, and when he returned in the evening, the snow storm overtook him, and he could scarcely escape, his garments froze round his body, and he wandered he knew not whither: at length he reached a cave, and remained there for three days, until the storm abated. Thorodd having thus again failed to destroy the minstrel, invited Snorri Godi, his brother-in-law, in summer, and told him how much he was injured and insulted by Biorn, and that it behoved Snorri to destroy the evil.

Snorri Godi spread now the report that he was going down to his ship, but he rode back with his men to attack Biorn, and to destroy him; and he appointed Marr, his man, to give him the first wound. But Biorn, who was in the field, fashioning a dray with his long knife, saw Snorri and his men riding down from the hills, and recognised them; and he took his knife, and went to meet them as soon as he could, and he seized instantly the sleeve of Snorri with one hand, and held the knife in the other, so that he was able to strike Snorri to the heart, if he saw that it was necessary to his own safety. The hands of Marr fell, for he saw that if he attacked Biorn, the latter would immediately kill Snorri. Then Biorn said, "Neighbour Snorri, my attitude seems threatening to you, but I have reason to believe, that you have come with hostile intentions. But now, if you have any business to transact with me, transact it openly,—if you have none, swear peace!"

"Our meeting has so fallen out," answered Snorri, "that we shall this time separate as much in peace as we were before. I wish, however, to obtain a promise from you, that you will abstain from visiting Thurid; for, if you persist in this, there never can be. any sincere friendship between us." Biorn answered, "This will I promise, and I will observe it, but I do not know how I shall be able to observe it, while I and Thurid live in the same land."

"There is nothing so important detaining you here," answered Snorri, "as to prevent your going to some other country." "That is true," answered Biorn, "and so let it be; let our interview close with this promise, that neither you nor Thorodd shall have cause to take any umbrage from my visits to Thurid in time to come."

They parted. The next day Biorn rode down to Krossahaven, and engaged his passage in a ship for the same summer. They set sail with a north-east wind, which prevailed during that summer, and of the fate of that ship nothing was heard more.

Some thirty years later, Gudleif, the merchant of Stromfiord, in Iceland, in his return from Dublin, fell in with north-east and east winds, and was driven far into the ocean, so that no land was seen. Many prayers were offered by Gudleif and his men, that they might escape their perils, till at length they saw land. It was of great extent and they knew not what land it was.

Not willing to struggle any longer with the perils of the ocean, they cast anchor; but when they had gone ashore, they were seized and fettered by the natives, and brought before an assembly, where the natives were disputing what should be done with them; they gathered, that some were for slaying them, others for distributing them among the different villages and making slaves of them. Whilst the debate was going on, a large body of men came riding along with a banner elevated in the midst, and under the banner they saw a man, tall, and of military deportment, aged and grey-headed, and all the natives treated him with great respect. He accosted Gudleif in the Norse tongue, and having ascertained that he was an Icelander, the chief asked him whether Snorri Godi was alive still, and his sister Thurid, and en-quired with a special interest into every particular relating to them.

The natives growing impatient that some decision should be come to, as to the fate of the strangers, the old man took with him twelve of the natives, and talked with them apart for a long time. At length he returned, and said, "the natives have left the matter to my decision, I will now therefore permit you to depart, and although the summer is far advanced, I recommend you to depart immediately, for these people are faithless, and difficult to deal with, and they think that they have now been deprived of their just right."

Then Gudleif enquired, "Whom shall we report, if we ever reach our native land again, to have done us this great favour?" "That I will not tell you," answered he, "for I am unwilling that any of my relatives and friends should come hither, and meet with such a fate as you would have met, had I not saved you. Age creeps upon me now so fast, that I almost expect each day to be my last; and then, there are in this land men of greater power than myself, and these would not grant peace or safety to any foreigner."

Before their departure he pulled a golden ring from off his finger, and gave it to Gudleif, saying, "If fortune grant that you reach Iceland, give this ring to Thurid of Froda." Gudleif enquired, "who shall I say was the sender of this precious gift?" He answered, "Say that he sent it, who loved the lady of Froda better than her brother the Godi of Helgafal." He gave to him also a sword for Thurid's son, and when Gudleif and his party had reached Iceland, he delivered the ring and the sword, and it was generally thought, that there could be no doubt

the man they had seen was the Scald Biorn Breid-
vikingakappi, and the country where they had been
Huitramannaland, the land south of Vinland.*

* I am indebted for the facts mentioned in this Appendix principally to ' The Discovery of America by the Northmen in the Tenth
Century ;' by Joshua Toulmin Smith, who has translated the documents published by the Northern Antiquarian Society of Copenhagen, with a most learned and lively Commentary, in dialogical
form.

END OF VOL. I.